AIRCAM/**AIRWAR** SERIES EDITOR: MAI

LUFTWAFFE FIGHTER UNITS
OPE, SEPTEMBER 1939 – JUNE 1941

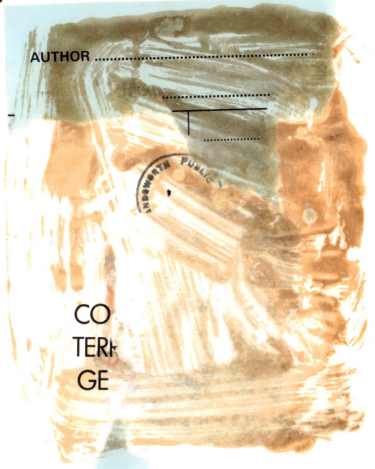

OSPREY PUBLISHING LONDON

Published in 1977 by
Osprey Publishing Ltd
Member company of tne George Philip Group
12–14 Long Acre, London WC2E 9LP
© Copyright 1977 Osprey Publishing Ltd

ISBN 0 85045 204 X

All photographs, unless specifically credited otherwise, are
reproduced by courtesy of E. J. Creek.

Filmset by BAS Printers Limited, Wallop, Hampshire, England
Printed in Hong Kong

PRELUDE

More than a decade before the first flight trials of the aircraft that would make the German fighter arm supreme in the opening rounds of World War II, the *Reichswehr* Government had laid the foundations for a new air force following the unacceptable Allied decisions of 1918. Fostered throughout the 1920s, the clandestine 'black Luftwaffe' was given a new impetus when Hitler came to power in 1933. Hermann Göring took overall control of aviation matters as air minister, and Secretary of State Erhard Milch was given responsibility for forging the raw material into the future instrument of war. On 26 February 1935 Hitler and Göring signed the decree that established the *Reichsluftwaffe* as the third element of the German armed forces, and on 14 March it was announced that the first fighter wing had been created, under the title *Jagdgeschwader Richthofen*. Young Germans, many of whom had received some flying training in the various civilian facilities located all over the country, could now openly join the air force.

Following his acceptance as a prospective pilot, an individual would receive basic training at a *Fliegerausbildungsregimenter,* where he would undergo a demanding programme of parades, drill, sport, lectures and so forth before being recommended for flying instruction. He would then transfer to a *Flugzeugführerschule* (FFS), in which there were two basic classes. An aspiring pilot would go to the first, the A/B school where, after an intensive grounding in theory, he would take about 100 hours flying training. This enabled him to gain his B1 and B2 certificates, qualifying him for high altitude and cross-country flights, instrument landings and testifying to his ability to cope with emergencies.

Fighter pilots were then posted to a *Jagdfliegerschule* (JFS) to prepare for further instruction before being transferred to an operational unit. General military training continued, interspersed with operational flying training, first on second-line aircraft and then on the Bf109—after an extensive ground conversion course to enable students to know the demanding fighter as well as possible before taking it up for the first time. A new pilot, with the rank of *Fähnrich* (flight cadet), would then transfer to an *Ergänzungs* (replacement) detachment of an operational squadron to await his first combat mission.

As the Luftwaffe's premier fighter unit, JG 132 *Richthofen* was given the task of bringing the Bf109 to operational status. First examples of the Bf109B-2 were delivered in 1937, the recipients being the I *Gruppe* at Doberitz, near Berlin. However, Nazi support for Franco's Nationalists soon meant a change from peaceful conversion training to front-line combat in Spain.

Their training having bred a fine spirit of both individuality and team-work, German fighter pilots

1. Messerschmitt Bf109E-1 photographed just before the outbreak of war. The all-over green colour scheme, narrow insignia crosses, and central placing of the tail swastika are typical of the period. The nose insignia appears to be that of I/JG 1—later, III/JG 27.

in Spain were quick to re-appraise the combat tactics they had been taught to use, and to tailor them to the modern machines they were flying. It was found that the close, wing-to-wing 'V' formations of World War I vintage left little room for manoeuvre in a fast fighter, and a new formation was introduced that was to be adopted by virtually every other air force in the world—the *Schwarm* or 'finger four'. Perfected by the brilliant Werner Mölders, this mutual protection formation was based on the *Rotte* of two aircraft. While the leader navigated and covered his wingman, the latter guarded his leader. The *Schwarm*, two formations of

two, flew with each machine positioned as though at the tips of the fingers of an outstretched hand, each maintaining 200 yards separation, the turning circle of the Bf109. Each *Schwarm* flew at a different altitude to give good cross-cover in all directions and make the best use of available firepower.

With the valuable combat reports from Spain showing where the Bf109 design could be improved, development proceeded, the Bf109C and D variants entering service in 1938. That year also saw the twin-engined Bf110B-1 make its service debut, to be followed by the Bf110C, both models having a forward-firing armament of four 7.9 mm machine guns and two 20 mm MG FF cannon. In 1938 the Bf109E-0 was evaluated by the Luftwaffe, whereupon production concentrated on the Bf109E-1, the majority of which were armed with two wing-mounted 20 mm MG FF cannon, with a pair of MG 17 machine guns in the upper decking of the fuselage nose. Some Bf109E-1s reached Spain before the termination of hostilities in March 1939.

By the end of 1938, the first Bf109Es were in the hands of JG 132 and throughout the spring and summer of 1939 the type entered service with feverish haste as new units were formed. By September, fifteen *Gruppen* had taken it on strength: I(J)/LG 2, I/JG 3, I/JG 20, I and II/JG 26, I/JG 51, I/JG 52, I and II/JG 53, I/JG 70, I/JG 71, I/JG 76, I and II/JG 77 and II/JG 1. Six *Gruppen*—I/JG 1, I/JG 2, I/JG 21, I/ZG 2, I/ZG 52 and II/ZG—retained the Bf109D-1. The intention had been to equip nine *Zerstörergruppen* with the Bf110, but only three had received it by the outbreak of war—I/(Z)LG 1, I/ZG 1 and I/ZG 76.

POLAND

The uncertain reaction by the Western allies to a German violation of Poland prompted caution in the deployment of the Luftwaffe fighter arm for Hitler's first demonstration of *Blitzkrieg*. Consequently, less then 200 Bf109s were included in the order of battle for the attack, the greater part of the *Jagdverbande* strength being retained to meet any threat from the

Definition of Terms

In the spring of 1939, the Luftwaffe chain of command was streamlined to handle the number of new units that had been formed, and were forming, in the last eighteen months or so. Each flying unit became subordinated to three new operational commands known as *Luftflotten* (Air Fleets). There were four main *Luftflotten* by March 1939, numbered 1 to 4 and commanded by *Gen.* Kesselring, Felmy, Sperrle and Löhr, respectively. Each had a separate operational area: *Luftflotte* 1, with headquarters in Berlin, covered eastern and northern Germany; *Luftflotte* 2 (HQ Brunswick) covered north-west Germany; *Luftflotte* 3 (HQ Munich) covered south-west Germany; and *Luftflotte* 4 (HQ Vienna) covered south-east Germany, Czechoslovakia and Austria.

Within each *Luftflotte*, administrative work was undertaken by a *Luftgau* (Air District), the operational organization being the *Fliegerkorps* (formerly *Fliegerdivision*), which were assigned to each *Luftflotten* according to operational requirements; a typical *Luftflotte* establishment was two *Fliegerkorps*, each with three complete *Geschwader* of bomber, dive bomber or fighter *Gruppen*, plus specialized *Gruppen* or *Staffeln*. The *Gruppe* was the basic Luftwaffe flying unit comprising some 30–40 aircraft, or the strength of three *Staffeln*, which were in turn sub-divided into groups of four aircraft (in the case of fighter units) to form a *Schwarm* or two, a *Rotte*. Usually each *Gruppe* and *Geschwader* had a headquarters flight known as the *Stab*. The leaders of the various units (*Geschwaderkommodore*, *Gruppenkommandeur*, etc) flew their own aircraft, which formed the *Geschwader* or *Gruppe Stabschwarm*. Each *Geschwader* usually had a *Stabschwarm* and three or four *Gruppen*, which were identified by Roman numerals: I *Gruppe* would have *Staffeln* 1 to 3, II *Gruppe Staffeln* 4 to 6, and so on; Arabic numerals always identified *Staffeln*. Thus, a complete *Geschwader* could number over 100 aircraft, but this figure varied (often considerably) depending on attrition, losses, serviceability and so on.

west, particularly from Britain or France. To meet any Polish attack from the east, 24 *Staffeln* of fighters were held in readiness in Germany. For the Polish campaign therefore, the units committed to action were I(J)/LG 2, II/ZG 1 and I/JG 21 with the Bf109E (the latter group still operating a number of Bf109Ds), I/ZG 2 and I/JG 1 with Bf109Ds, plus the strength of the three Bf110 *Gruppen* which were destined to see the most air combat with the Polish Air Force in the coming weeks. Luftwaffe fighter strength was thus 210 fighters and 1,371 bomber, ground-attack and reconnaissance types, the bulk of this force coming under the jurisdiction of Kesselring's *Luftflotte* 1 (east) and Lohr's *Luftflotte* 4 (south-east). To oppose this formidable number of aircraft, most of which were considerably superior to their equivalents anywhere in the world, the Polish Air Force had 159 obsolescent PZL P.11 and P.7 fighters.

The war in the air began at 04.00 hours on 1 September, with attacks on the Vistula Bridge at Tczew and a number of Polish airfields, including Kraków. Other targets were hammered during the day and it soon became clear that the Polish defences were no match for German tactics and equipment.

Luftwaffe priorities for the successful sub-jugation of Poland were: destruction of the enemy air force, co-operation with the army and navy in their operations by attacks on troop concentrations and lines of communication behind the front, and attacks on 'centres of enemy strength', i.e. industrial and population centres. The speed of the advance on the ground meant, however, that all three target categories could be attacked simultaneously.

A morning raid by the He111s of II/LG 1 on Warsaw—Okecie airfield achieved little owing to poor visibility, and recorded the first clash with enemy fighters. In a forty-minute running fight, the first major aerial engagement of the war, six German bombers went down for the loss of four Polish fighters, two to bomber gunners and two to the escorting Bf110s of I(Z)/LG 1; the *Gruppe* CO, *Maj.* Grabmann, was wounded.

A second attack on the Polish capital developed in the late afternoon, when KG 27's He111s arrived

2. Bf109E-1 bearing the bow-and-arrow insignia of 7 Staffel, JG 51 being refuelled from a bowser during an exercise immediately before the invasion of Poland.

over the city at 17.30 hours after a 470-mile flight from their home bases. Both Bf109s and the Bf110s of I(Z)/LG 1 provided the fighter escort, led by *Hptm.* Schleif in place of *Maj.* Grabmann. Some thirty PZLs rose to intercept and in the ensuing air battle, the German formations were scattered so that their bombs did little damage. A number of PZLs were

3. Messerschmitt of 7/JG 51, bearing the Staffel insignia on the nose and white fuselage markings including the III Gruppe symbol aft of the cross, overflown by a Rotte of Bf109E-1s of the same unit.

4. Immaculate Bf109E-1 of II/JG 54 in a peaceful 'Phoney War' setting—note engine crank-handle in place in the side of the cowling.

shot down by the Luftwaffe fighter escort and one Bf109 was lost when it was rammed by a P.11.

Polish pilots tended to respect the concentrated fire from the Bf110's battery of nose guns, the Bf109 being regarded 'rather lightly'. This view was substantiated by LG 1's twenty-five aerial victories in the campaign. Contemporary Polish accounts indicate that it was the Luftwaffe's sheer technical superiority in all types of aircraft that was the biggest shock, rather than the numbers encountered. None of the Polish fighters had cannon armament and the PZL P.11's top speed of approximately 240 mph was comparable only to that of the German bombers. With their considerable speed margin, the Luftwaffe fighters could engage on their own terms and break off combat at will.

If they were at a disadvantage in the air, the Polish fighters' ground support was hardly any brighter; the lack of an effective early-warning system spread slim resources dangerously thin and often hampered interception. The PAF was not destroyed on the ground, only because it managed to disperse its fighter force to well-camouflaged emergency airfields. Although many aircraft were disabled by bombing and strafing, small numbers of fighters continued to intercept. When contact was made, their slashing attacks usually meant the loss of German bombers, the armament of which frequently proved to be inadequate.

On 2 September, 2 *Staffel* of ZG 76 engaged in a violent air battle over the town of Lodz, losing three of its number for two PZLs, although only two Bf110s were claimed by the Poles. One of the PZLs fell to Helmut Lent—the first of his eventual 110 victories during the war. A number of high-scoring Luftwaffe pilots gained their first kills over Poland, including Hans Philipp of I/ZG 76, Erwin Clausen (3/LG 2), Gustav Rödel (I/JG 21—later III/JG 54) and Gordon Gollob (I/ZG 76).

The Bf109Ds of I/ZG 2 achieved considerable success on 3 September. Based at Gross-Stein near Oppeln in Upper Silesia, the unit was commanded by *Hptm.* Hannes Gentzen, who recorded some of his combat experiences in *Luftwaffe Schagt Zui* by Peter Supf, published in Berlin in 1939:

'The hardest part is tracking down the Polish fighters—bringing them down is quite a bit easier. The Pole is a master at concealment and the green-brown camouflage of [his] aircraft is excellent. Then too, the Poles often place their machines so skilfully in a row along wooded roads that they are difficult to spot.

'On the occasion of my *Staffel*'s first air combat, we also had our greatest success. We were flying near Lodz at about 1,000 m altitude, widely echeloned, when we saw two Polish fighters in front of us, one of which was at a higher altitude. Part of the *Staffel* dived downward. I myself attacked one. My shots must have hit his motor, because he immediately went into a downward glide. We followed him closely and saw to our amazement that the spot on which he intended to land was a well-camouflaged operational airfield (believed to be Widzew). This was a complete surprise! We would never have discovered it had not the runway acted as a guide. The damaged aircraft nosed-over on landing and burst into flames. The pilot ran for cover.'

This particular account goes on to describe the destruction of a further nine Polish fighters dispersed on the airfield in strafing attacks, although the claim appears to be at variance with Polish records, which accept the loss of two airborne P.11s in the circumstances described, plus

five by strafing, but on 4 September—*Hptm*. Gentzen's report was for the 3rd. Nevertheless, the quoted passage does serve to emphasize the Luftwaffe's singular lack of success in locating Polish operational fighter airfields. Other details in the report showed the performance margin the German fighters enjoyed:

'Due to the great speed of our machines, dogfights occur very seldom. Either you're in a good position and attack at high speed, preferably out of the sun, or off you go in search of a better target. On the first day of the battle, we escorted our bombers and *Stukas* to protect them or we flew out in front of them and cleared the air. [Based] around Annaburg in Upper Silesia, there were five dive-bomber *Gruppen* and one *Schlacht* and one *Zerstörergruppe*. Our *Staffeln* alternated in escorting the various units; we flew from morning until evening.'

Dealing with the fighting in the latter days of September, Gentzen's account mentions ground-strafing techniques:

'Since by then Polish fighters seldom showed themselves, we looked for other targets. Shooting up locomotives developed into a particular speciality with us. For this we would

5. Factory line-up of Bf110C heavy fighters, the two nearest machines still in manufacturer's radio call-sign markings, and—puzzlingly—what appears to be natural metal finish.

be in *Ketten* [formation] down to two or three metres above the ground. While one would shoot at the locomotive, the other two would rake the train with their machine guns in order to prevent anyone getting off and making use of his weapons.'

As a result of their train-strafing success in Poland, 3 Staffel of ZG 76 (Bf110) adopted the insignia of a locomotive.

The morning of 3 September saw further bitter resistance to the bombing raids on Warsaw (the Luftwaffe's Operation *Seaside*), with three of the fighter escort shot down. By the 4th, with the Polish armies in retreat, targets were troop concentrations, rail links, roads and so forth, the *Jagdflieger* becoming increasingly involved in ground-strafing work.

Bf109s tangled with P.11s on the morning of the 5th; two of the Heinkels they were escorting were shot down and two Bf110s were also destroyed in a violent midday air battle over the outskirts of Warsaw. In most of these encounters, the Polish fighters sustained damage, a fact which was eventually to prove decisive—there were simply no

6. Messerschmitt Bf110C Zerstörer undergoing a major overhaul. Such technical facilities would be sorely missed during the lightning advances from airfield to airfield which characterized Luftwaffe operations in 1940.

7. The nose-battery of the Bf110 was massive for its day— two 7.92 mm machine guns and two 20 mm cannon. Göring's enthusiasm for the heavy fighter concept failed to take into account, however, the lack of manoeuvrability which usually prevented Bf110 pilots from bringing their impressive armament to bear. (Via R. L. Ward)

reserves to replace those machines forced to remain on the ground for repairs.

The first six days of the Polish campaign cost the Luftwaffe over a hundred aircraft for the destruction of seventy-nine Polish machines; six Bf109s and four Bf110s were lost out of a total of forty-two aircraft destroyed in the air battles over Warsaw, where the Polish defence was at its most aggressive. After 7 September, German command of the air was never seriously challenged by the PAF, although the entire campaign eventually cost the Luftwaffe 564 aircraft, including sixty-seven Bf109s and twelve Bf110s, twelve of the former and nine of the latter being claimed by Polish fighters. The balance reflects a high attrition rate in a short period of operations, but the sortie rate was considerable and there were many losses due to non-operational causes. Victory in Poland had been unable to give the *Jagdflieger* a clear indication of the capabilities of their aircraft or the soundness of their tactics. The Bf109 did not meet an enemy fighter anywhere near its equal and the Bf110 crews were dangerously deluded into thinking that their machine could also overcome fighter opposition.

At 11:00 hours on the third day of the Polish campaign, Britain and France declared war on Germany, and within hours, the first RAF operational sorties of the war were flown to photograph intended naval targets. The *Jagdflieger* made contact with British aircraft for the first time on 4 September, when a Bf109 shot down a Wellington during an attack on the *Scharnhorst* and *Gneisenau* lying off Brunsbüttel.

Four days later, the German fighter arm suffered its first casualties in the West when two of JG 2's Bf109Es were shot down by five Curtiss Hawk 75As of the Armée de l'Air's *Groupe de Chasse* II/4 over the Maginot Line. Then, on 18 December, guided by an early example of *Freya* early-warning radar, the fighters intercepted twenty-two Wellingtons bent on armed reconnaissance of German naval units in the Shillig Roads. To meet such an eventuality, JG 1 at Jever in East Friesland had nearly a hundred fighters under its command and the Bf109Cs of 10 (*Nacht*)/JG 26, Bf109Es of II and III/JG 77, Bf109Bs of II/ZG 1 and the Bf110Cs of 1 and 2 *Staffel* I/ZG 76 were more than enough to hack down twelve of the lightly-armed British bombers.

An early victim fell to a beam attack by *Oblt*. Steinhoff's Bf109, against which the Wellington was defenceless. *Ltn*. Helmut Lent of I/ZG 76 shot down three and others fell to Bf110 pilots; Wolfgang Falck, *Staffelkapitän* of 2 *Staffel*, dispatched two before his machine was forced to return to base, damaged by defensive fire from the bombers. Two Bf109s were shot down, one pilot being lost. Although full of praise for the courage of the British bomber crews, Carl Schumacher, *Kommandeur* of II/JG 77, could not help but comment on their sacrifice:

'It was criminal folly on the part of the enemy to fly at 4,000–5,000 metres in a cloudless sky with perfect visibility . . . After such losses it is assumed that the enemy will not give the *Geschwader* any more opportunities of practice-shooting at Wellingtons.' Schumacher was proved right. After the 18 December débâcle—and the loss of some forty aircraft to all combat causes, over half to fighters, in the first three months of the war—the RAF heavy-bomber offensive was conducted at night.

SCANDINAVIA AND THE LOW COUNTRIES

During the first winter of the war, Luftwaffe fighter units began to receive a new model of the Bf109, the E-3. With its heavy armament of two cannon and two machine guns, a maximum speed of 310 mph at 25,000 ft and a rate of climb of 1,340 ft per minute, the aircraft had few peers in the world—there was certainly no fighter based on the continent of Europe that could match it in the hands of a good pilot. Thus, as both sides on the Western Front made tentative incursions into each other's air space, mainly to gather intelligence data, the *Jagdflieger* had every confidence that their machines could meet any eventuality. On occasions, both the Bf109 and 110 made contact with the British and French, and Blenheims were among their first kills of 1940. In Germany, new Luftwaffe units became

8. The pilot of an 'Emil' of Jagdgeschwader 2 'Richthofen' adjusts his helmet while his mechanic holds his seat-straps ready. The colour of their fatigue overalls earned Luftwaffe groundcrew the nickname of 'black men'.

operational during the bleak winter months, among them JG 27 under the command of *Obstltn*. Max Ibel.

The weather closed in on 14 January, extreme temperatures and heavy snow halting all air operations over most of Europe until 18 February, when both sides resumed air reconnaissance. Prior to the cold spell, on 10 January, Reinhard Seiler, a *Staffelkapitän* of I/JG 54 scored his first victory. On 3 March the Bf109s tangled with Hurricanes of the RAF's Advanced Air Striking Force, the combat resulting in the loss of one Messerchmitt for two Hurricanes damaged. The British squadrons in

9. Pleasing plan-view of a Bf109E; in this case the high individual number painted on a coloured band round the rear fuselage indicates service with a training unit. (Via R. L. Ward)

10. The cockpit of the Bf109E—after modifications by its British captors, including the removal of the reflector gunsight and the fitting of a new airspeed indicator. The cockpit of the little 'Emil' was cramped even for a man of average build. (Imperial War Museum)

France at that time were equipped with a motley collection of Hurricanes, some with fixed-pitch wooden airscrews which did not bestow an outstanding performance. These early machines also lacked adequate armour protection for the pilot and there were examples with outdated ring-and-bead gunsights. Hurricanes fitted with variable-pitch, three-bladed, metal propellers were 20 mph faster but the German fighter pilots did not generally regard the type as a difficult adversary. The Bf109 could still use its superior diving speed to break off combat with British fighters, and its pilots had the comforting knowledge that direct fuel injection would not result in an engine cut-out when the stick was pushed hard forward.

On 31 March, the increased tempo of the air war was marked by the loss of three Bf110s during the period immediately prior to the first German attack in the West. Armée de l'Air MS. 406s engaged five Bf109s and shot down two for the loss of one of their number.

On 9 April 1940 the months of relative inactivity, known as 'Sitzkreig' to the Germans and 'Phoney War' to the Allies, came to a sudden end with the simultaneous invasion of Norway and Denmark by German naval and air units. Operation Weserübung—Excercise Weser—was undertaken principally to deny Britain the use of Norwegian waters and airfields in that part of northern Europe from which she could effectively seal off the entire North Sea from Scapa Flow to Stavanger.

Fighter support for Luftwaffe anti-shipping and troop transport operations in the Norwegian campaign was limited, only II/JG 77's Bf109E-3s and some 70 Bf110s of I/ZG 1 and I/ZG 76 taking part. The long-range Bf110 was ideally suited to the distances involved, the former unit then being based at Barth and the latter at Westerland. Such was the success of the German attack, however, that both Zerstörer units were able to use Aalborg and Stavanger airfields by the evening of the first day of the operation. Bf110s also strafed Vaerlose, destroying five Fokker D.XXIs on the ground shortly before the Danes capitulated.

A primary objective of Weserübung was the capture of four main airfields in Norway: Aalborg—East and West in Northern Jutland; Oslo—Fornebu, intended as a base for offensive sorties against the Norwegian capital; and Stavanger—Sola on the south-west coast for defensive operations against the British fleet. Trondheim-Vaernes airfield and the small landing strip at Kristiansand were also to be captured, the latter falling on the second day of the attack and being quickly occupied by the three Staffeln of II/JG 77.

Paratroops were to take the key airfields and the early morning of 9 April saw Ju52s heading for Fornebu, escorted by eight Bf110s of I/ZG 76 under Hptm. Hansen. Low overcast caused the fighter and transports to become separated and at 08.45 hours, Hansen's aircraft were over Fornebu. There were now six Bf110s, two having fallen to the guns of Royal Norwegian Air Force Gladiators. At 09.05 the

first of the Ju52s arrived and made to land, only to sheer off under fire from the airfield perimeter. Hansen's aircraft were short of fuel and, with three of his Bf110s now flying on only one of their engines, he ordered *Ltn.* Lent to take his machine in. Lent, who had earlier destroyed his fifth enemy aircraft in combat with Gladiators, lowered his wheels and flaps and made his approach. Hansen led his remaining three aircraft in a strafing attack on gun emplacements on the airfield perimeter as Lent's Bf110 crash-landed. By 09.19, with all the Bf110s on the ground and the rest of the Ju52s having arrived, including the *Zerstörer* unit's own transport, the airfield had been secured. It was with some pride that Hansen radioed, 'Fornebu is in our hands. I/ZG 76.' No German troops had been needed to capture the vital airfield, but at Stavanger, after cloud again scattered the transports, the planned paratroop drop was made just after 09.00.

Bad weather had forced two Bf110s of 3/ZG 76 to return home and so, to cover the Stavanger force, Gordon Gollob had only two aircraft with which to strafe a pair of gun positions on the airfield boundary; but once the paratroops landed and went into action, it took only thirty minutes to secure the airfield.

German naval units were still top of RAF Bomber Command's target list at that time and on 12 April, a dozen Hampdens struck at the *Scharnhorst* and *Gneisenau*. The formation was intercepted by BF109s and 110s and chased out to sea; six of the Hampdens were shot down. Sporadic fighting continued in Norway until 3 May, by which time

Luftwaffe activity had tailed off. I/ZG 1 had withdrawn to Germany to prepare for the main offensive in the West a few days' hence.

Before the assault of 10 May, the Allied air forces had been able to test-fly the Luftwaffe's much vaunted single-seat fighter for themselves. On 22 November 1939 a Bf109E-3 of I/JG 76 had landed by mistake near Woerth, Bas-Rhin, some twelve miles (20 km) inside French territory. The valuable prize was transported to Orleans-Bricy for trials by the Armée de l'Air and thence to England, where it was flown at A&AEE Boscombe Down.

Detailed reports following a number of flights showed that the Bf109E was superior to the Hurricane Mk I on most counts except low-altitude manoeuvrability and radius of turn at all altitudes, but that the Spitfire Mk I had the edge above 20,000 ft. The German fighter could usually lose both Spitfire and Hurricane in a steep-angle dive, however, due to the advantage of direct fuel injection for its DB 601 engine.

Good points of the Bf109 were summarized thus: high top speed and excellent rate of climb, good low-speed control, gentle stalling characteristics even under high g loads and good engine performance, which was not lost immediately under negative g. Bad points were: ailerons and other

13. Framed by the standard of the Luftwaffe Jagdverbande and a pair of tripod-mounted binoculars, this Bf109E is thought to have served with I/JG 2. A colour print shows the '3' to have been black, and the insignia below the cockpit appears to be a personal 'Popeye the Sailorman' motif. The colour-scheme now features pale blue right up to the fuselage spine. (Via R. L. Ward).

14. Rare close-formation flying shot of four Bf109E-1s of 1/JG 2 'Richthofen'; the 'Bonzo Dog' emblem of the Staffel is just visible in front of the intake on the side of the cowling of 'white 7', and the red 'R' of the Geschwader emblem appears beneath the windscreens of all four aircraft. Note the pale blue paintwork of the undersides taken even higher on the rear fuselage, limiting the green splinter camouflage to the extreme top decking.

flying surfaces were too heavy at high speeds, the turning circle was poor and the machine had a tendency to stall readily (though not viciously) at g due to high wing loading; the ailerons snatched as the wing slats opened, and the lack of a rudder trimmer restricted the ability to bank left at high speeds.

These reports were available to both the British and French before the invasion, although some die-hard Frenchmen believed that their fighters could prevent a débâcle in the air. That illusion was about to be shattered in six weeks' bloody fighting.

Concurrent with the attack on France, the Germans wanted to secure their northern flank by invading the neutral territories of Holland and Belgium. On the morning of 10 May the Luftwaffe bombed airfields in Belgium, Holland and France, and German pioneer troops made a brilliant glider-borne assault on the main Belgian defence line centred on Fort Eben Emaël. By the afternoon of the 11th, Panzer columns, under an umbrella of *Stukas*, were across the strategic waterways of the Albert Canal and River Maas.

A full-scale attack in the west was a calculated risk for the Luftwaffe; the operation had to be completed quickly if replacement aircraft were to

keep the units up to strength. Nevertheless, the *Luftwaffe-generalstab* committed a sizeable force, including 16 *Gruppen* of fighters, drawn from JG 1, 2, 3, 21, 26, 27, 51, 53 and 54, all equipped with the Bf109E, plus nine *Gruppen* of Bf110s from LG 1, ZG 1 and ZG 76—1,016 single-seat and 248 twin-engined fighters within an overall total of 3,902 aircraft available for the operation.

In Holland, the *Luchtvaartafdeling*—Netherlands Army Air Service—was fully alerted before the assault and had occupied the airfields of Amsterdam-Schipol, Bergen, De Kooy, Ypenburg and Waalhaven. There were 132 serviceable aircraft, the most modern fighter being the Fokker G.1A, twenty-three of which were on hand; the most numerous fighter type was the rugged little Fokker D.XXI, of which there were twenty-eight available on 10 May.

As the smoke and dust from the Luftwaffe's bombs cleared, the first waves of Ju52s dropped their paratroops on the three main airfields of the

15. With the French armistice signed, Bf110s could fly over Paris with impunity. These four Bf110Cs bear the codes of Lehrgeschwader 1 (L1), the yellow individual code letters ('C', 'A', 'K' and 'L' visible) and the Staffel code 'L' of 3(Z)/LG 1. The colour schemes are interesting: 'K' is still in overall dark green, but the others wear the later scheme with pale blue fuselage sides mottled over with green and grey, and a splinter pattern of two greens on the wings and fuselage top decking. The mottling appears to have been carried out at unit level and with a fine free hand—horizontal streaks were definitely non-regulation! (Bildarchiv)

Hague and the vital Moerdijk Bridge over the Maas near Rotterdam. Waalhaven airfield was quickly taken to serve as a base for men and supplies. To escort them, the Ju52s operating over Waalhaven had four Bf110s of I/ZG 1 under *Hptm.* Werner Streib. His aircraft had taken off from Gutersloh at 07.30 hours and arrived over the Dutch airfield at 10.00 hours. With the airfield in German hands, Streib's machines had little difficulty in fending off an attack by six Blenheims of No. 600 Sqn. RAF,

16. Aircraft of III/JG 51 on a French airfield. Note the Gruppe emblem beneath the cockpit of the furthest aircraft—the chevron and circle motif in front of the fuselage cross indicates the machine of the Gruppe Technical Officer. In the foreground is the nose emblem of 8 Staffel, a black cat on a white disc.

which strafed the Ju52s. Streib shot down the first Blenheim and others were quickly dispatched; only one of the bombers returned to Manston.

German casualties were considerable at Ypenburg and Valkenburg; Dutch anti-aircraft fire was intense and fighters repeatedly strafed the Ju52s that had put down on the beaches north of the Hague. Bf109s sustained losses helping to keep the

Dutch fighters away from the vulnerable troop-carriers, four being shot down by the D.XXIs of 1e Ja V.A. from De Kooy. One Fokker was shot down and one damaged. At Schipol, 2e Ja V.A. lost two Fokkers when the airfield came under attack, and the 109s bounced 5e Ja V.A. as it was barely airborne, inflicting heavy losses. By the fifth day of the fighting, the Dutch were still capable of offensive operations in the air, but, with the bombing of Rotterdam, the nation sued for peace. Throughout the campaign the Luftwaffe had systematically attacked troop concentrations, lines of communication and strongpoints virtually at will.

Events in Belgium followed the now-familiar *Blitzkrieg* pattern. With only eleven Hurricane Mk Is, fifteen Gladiators and thirty-one Fiat CR.42s, the fighter arm of the *Aeronautique Militaire* had even less chance of resisting than the Dutch. Luftwaffe strikes virtually wiped out the Belgian air force on the ground. At Beauechain, 1eme *Escadrille* lost all its Hurricanes and 2eme *Esc,* eleven of its Gladiators, while at Brustem, sixteen CR.42s were destroyed. One of the Gladiators that managed to take off had the dubious honour of being the first aerial victory for I/JG 27, when it fell to the guns of Heino Echer's Bf109E near Tienen. The remnants of the Belgian fighter force retreated into France.

FRANCE

On 10 May there were 552 serviceable fighters available to the Armée de l'Air, deployed throughout four zonal commands, where each *Groupement* had the task of supporting the armies in the field.

17. This Bf109E, an early victim of the Battle of Britain, has an interesting mottle of green on the cowling only. Since the wing-tips are painted in a light colour (probably white, indicating I Gruppe, to judge by the lack of a Gruppe emblem behind the fuselage cross) it seems likely that the cowling was also painted white originally, and later over-sprayed for some reason.

18. Messerschmitt shooting up a barrage balloon over Dover in August 1940—the balloons were favourite 'targets of opportunity' for German pilots.

19. Luftwaffe second lieutenant in flying blouse (right) accepts a light from another officer (note piped sidecap) in front of a damaged Bf109E. A pile of sandbags supports the centre-section, and the starboard oleo leg is badly distorted.

20. Well-known but pleasing photo of Bf110Cs of the fighter-bomber unit Erprobungsgruppe 210, which specialized in pin-point fighter-bomber raids on selected targets during the Battle of Britain. The Gruppe code was S9; the emblem—a red 'England' in a yellow bomb-sight on a white shield—is visible on the nose. (Joos)

Although the Dewoitine D.520 was the most modern fighter, with a top speed of 334 mph and an armament of one 20 mm cannon and four machine guns, only one *Groupe de Chasse* was equipped with it—a total of thirty-six machines. Most numerous French fighter was the MS.406, 278 of which were on hand, equipping eleven *Groupes*. It had a top speed of 304 mph and an armament of one 20 mm cannon and two machine guns.

There were 140 Bloch 151s and 152s in seven *Groupes*; top speeds were 276 and 288 mph respectively, armament being four machine guns, and one cannon and two machine guns. The American Curtiss Hawk 75A equipped four *Groupes*, with a total of ninety-eight aircraft. Highly manoeuvrable, the Hawk had a top speed of 313 mph and was armed with four 7.5 mm machine guns. In addition, the RAF had an average daily strength of forty Hurricanes and twenty Gladiators in France.

Although responsible for maintaining air superiority over a front of 175 miles, the *Jagdflieger* did not view the French campaign with undue trepi-

dation. A Bf109 pilot summed up the general feeling: 'Although prior to the start of the campaign of May 1940, no German pilot could make a comprehensive comparison between British and French fighters and the Bf109E, we firmly believed that we had the best aircraft available, based on comparative flying reports and an abundance of rumours.'

As the Wehrmacht smashed forward, ably supported by the Luftwaffe, suicidal Allied dive-bombing and strafing could do little to halt the tank columns. In the air, the *Jagdflieger* clashed with French fighters attempting to get at the bomber formations and there were casualties on both sides. On occasions, the *Kampfgeschwader* fought off these attacks by maintaining formation and making good use of defensive fire, although fighter escort was stepped up on the 11th, by which time the Armée de l'Air had lost a considerable number of aircraft. These losses were not caused only by destruction in the air; as had happened before, the German

21. A pilot of JG 53 'Pik As' recounts an obviously eventful sortie over the Channel to his comrades.

armoured columns moved so quickly that they produced widespread disorganization and break-down of communications. Many French fighters had to be abandoned as their airfields were overrun, and pilots flying sorties from a forward base could not be sure that it would still be in friendly hands when they returned. The few French fighters that did intercept German bombers were frequently badly deployed, and the standard of gunnery of their pilots was often very poor.

Whit Sunday, 12 May, was a day of considerable success for the *Jagdflieger*, the cream of whom were distributed throughout the famous units committed to the battle. JG 27 had I/JG 1 and I/JG 21 under its operational control at that time, its aircraft flying from München-Gladbach and Gymnich near Cologne to cover the 6th Army's breakthrough at Maastricht–Liège. Max Ibel the *Geschwader-*

kommodore, had eighty-five operational Bf109Es at his disposal. At dawn two *Staffeln* of I/JG 1 under Joachim Schlichting took off to give fighter cover over the bridges spanning the Maas and Albert Canal, which had been taken by the 6th Army. Considerable air activity was anticipated over the sector as the enemy strove to destroy the bridges.

At 06.00 hours, 1 *Staffel*, led by *Oblt.* Walter Adolph, sighted a formation of Blenheims of No. 139 Sqn. and attacked. Intent on their target, the British aircraft were surprised and seven of their number fell to the Bf109s. RAF Battles made their suicidal strike on the Albert Canal bridges later in the day, destroying one span of the Veldwezelt Bridge. Flying with 8 *Staffel* of the recently-formed III/JG 52, Günther Räll shot down a French Hawk 75, his first kill.

Intense air combat took place throughout the day; 3/JG 27 saw further action when *Hptm.* Adolf Galland, then *Geschwader Adjutant*, accompanied by Gustav Rodel, dived on eight Hurricanes. Two

22. Pair of Bf109E-3s of II/JG 3 'Udet' off the British coast. The pale blue sides and tail have been given a mottled overspray. The all-important wingman in each two-man Rotte was nicknamed 'Holzauge'—'Wooden eye'—or 'Katchmarek'—Polish for 'faithful servant'.

23. The running boar emblem of I/JG 52 on the cowling of a Bf109E brought down over Kent late in August 1940. The blue fuselage and tail surfaces have been oversprayed almost completely.

24, 25. Plt. Off. Wicks of No. 56 Sqn., RAF, examining the Bf109E-3 of 6/JG 51 which he shot down on 24 August 1940. The Gruppe badge is painted on the rear fuselage; three white 'kill bars' appear above the Werke Nr., 5587 on the fin.

26. One of the 16 Bf109Es lost by the Luftwaffe over England on 5 September 1940 was this E-4 of the Staff Flight, II/JG 3 'Udet'; the black and white shield outlined in red is the Gruppe emblem. Note 13 'kill' bars on the fin forward of the swastika. This is widely believed to have been the aircraft of the famous Luftwaffe escaper, Franz von Werra. (*Kent Messenger*)

went down under Galland's fire and he destroyed a third during another patrol near Tienen—the first of his 104 kills. It was nearly dark when the last of JG 27's machines landed, the wing having flown 340 sorties and claimed twenty-eight victories. Moving forward to Charleville in the Ardennes, the unit was engaged in operation *Abendssegen*, the interception of French fighters using the twilight hours to strafe German ground forces.

By taking their tanks into and through the 'impregnable' Ardennes, the Germans had reached the River Meuse in the Sedan sector by 12 May and, under cover of *Stuka* attacks that thoroughly demoralized the defence, had crossed and consolidated the bridgehead by the 13th. Too late, the

Allies flung in all available forces to plug the breach. All day the opposing air forces contested the sky over the front lines. *Fliegerkorps II*'s war diary called 14 May 'the day of the fighters'.

Among the successful Luftwaffe fighter units that day was JG 53, I *Gruppe* of which was commanded by Jan von Jansen. The wing scored thirty-nine victories, five falling to Hans-Karl Mayer, three to Hans Ohly. Werner Mölders, whose name would soon become synonomous with the *experten* of the Luftwaffe, also scored. His victory tally stood at twenty-five by 5 June, and at around 17.00 hours on that day he was part of a formation of forty Bf109s that bounced a mixed formation of Dewoitine D.520s of GCI/3 and II/7 over Compiègne; two of the French fighters fell before *Sous Lieutenant* Pomier-Layraques turned his machine into the Bf109s and hit Mölders's aircraft, forcing the German to bail out.

JG 53, under Hans-Jurgen von Cramon-Taubadel, claimed 39 victories for 14 May; and in 814 sorties, the German fighter pilots had taken the lion's

share of eighty-nine Allied aircraft destroyed in the Sedan sector of the front. Some sixty per cent of the RAF bombers sent into action failed to return, and the official British comment was 'No higher rate of loss in an operation of comparable size has ever been experienced by the RAF'. The German advance continued.

The Panzers rolled through France at such a rate that the Luftwaffe had some difficulty in keeping

27, 28. Two views of Bf110C-3 W. Nr. 1372, U8+HL of 3/ZG 26 'Horst Wessel' brought down at Lenham, Kent on 11 September 1940. The crew were Uffz. Krusphow (gunner) and Fw. Brinkmann (pilot)—from the condition of the machine it would seem probable that they survived to be captured. The code letter 'H' is in yellow; the nose and narrow fuselage band appear to be white, as a further identification of a I Gruppe aircraft in a Geschwader whose machines tended to use a number of different codes: U8 and E8 in I/ZG 26, 3U in the other two Gruppen. (*Kent Messenger*)

ahead of them for the necessary close support strikes. Operating farther and farther from their home bases and at times utilizing makeshift forward airstrips, the *Stuka* and fighter formations had to be supplied both by road and by Ju52 transports, which maintained a constant shuttle service to and from Germany. By 24 May German armour was at Gravelines, some twelve miles from Dunkirk and it was decided to move the Bf109s of I/JG 27 into St Omer, recently vacated by the RAF. But as the *Stab* flight, led by Max Ibel, approached to land, shells were still falling on the airfield from both the German and Allied lines. Down to their last drops of fuel, the fighters managed to make St Pol a few miles farther south. and their pilots quickly went into action, escorting bombers that were trying to prevent the evacuation of the BEF from Dunkirk.

By 1 June, nearly 70,000 men had been taken off the beaches. Taxed to near-exhaustion by the last few weeks' fighting, the Luftwaffe pilots tried their best to carry out a task that should obviously have been performed by ground forces. Saddled with the task of protecting the bombers, the *Jagdflieger* had also to face the first enemy fighter capable of besting their faithful 'Emils'—the Supermarine Spitfire. No less than fifteen of the nineteen Spitfire squadrons then operational in Fighter Command were committed to action over Dunkirk. While the *Stuka* and bomber *Geschwader* pounded the ships and waiting men, the fighters went down to strafe the columns of troops—a grim business for pilots used to regarding the enemy as a 'thing' rather than people. One pilot of JG 2 recorded what he felt about this part of the operation: 'I hated Dunkirk. It was just unadulterated killing. The beaches were jammed full of soldiers. I went up and down at three hundred feet "hosepiping".'

While Operation *Dynamo* went on, the Luftwaffe continued to sortie against French forces. In the early afternoon of 3 June, approximately 300 bombers of *Luftflotten* 2 and 3 carried out Operation *Paula*, a mass strike on French airfields around Paris. Under heavy escort from Bf109s and 110s, the bombers hit their targets hard; the fighters engaged a number of French aircraft, including three Bloch 152 units and part of a fourth entrusted with the defence of the city. Caught taking off by Bf109s, nine of the French fighters were destroyed for two bombers and two Messerschmitts lost.

The months ahead would give the *Jagdflieger* their toughest test; but even before the end came in France, there were times when German fighters sustained heavy losses to the hard-fighting Frenchmen. On 8 June, *Capt.* Wuillame of GC.I/2 used his MS.406 to deadly effect, destroying three Bf109s in the space of 15 seconds. Six Bf110s fell to an equal number of MS.406s in 20 seconds on 13 May.

Undoubtedly the best French fighter faced by the Luftwaffe was the Dewoitine D.520; fast and highly manoeuvrable, the D.520s gave a good account of themselves, despite being few in number. On 15 June, for example, out of a total of ten confirmed kills by pilots of GC.I/3, five plus three probables were Bf109s.

THE BRITISH ISLES

On 9 June German troops reached Paris as the battle for France neared its inevitable conclusion. Churchill, doing his best to stave off defeat, continued talks with General Weygand, during which he raised the question of the 400 Luftwaffe prisoners then held by the French. Weygand promised to deliver them into British hands, but fortunately for the Germans the transfer was never made.

As the Luftwaffe occupied airfields in France and Belgium, ground-support sorties continued; the Armée de l'Air and the RAF, operating from both the Continent and England, tried desperately to stem the tide of armour. The fighting lasted until 22 June, when the Armistice underscored once again the price of military unpreparedness in the face of a vigorous militaristic power.

29. The Geschwaderkommodore of ZG 26 'Horst Wessel' throughout the Battle of Britain was a one-legged World War I veteran, Obstltn. Joachim-Friedrich Hüth. In this photo he wears regulation Luftwaffe officer's service tunic, with collar patches and shoulder-straps of rank, and the peaked service cap. The Ritterkreuz hangs at his throat. (Gemeinschaft der Jagdflieger E.V.)

30. Indistinct but interesting snapshot of a Gruppe Technical Officer's Bf109E over the Channel during the Battle of Britain. The fuselage is almost completely mottled over; rudder and cowling either remain in pale blue, or have been oversprayed white or yellow as a Gruppe identification. The white cliffs of Dover are just visible in the original print. From the strut in the right hand corner, the photo appears to have been taken from an aircraft of a type which might well have appreciated an escort when venturing within sight of England!

As replacement aircraft brought Luftwaffe units back up to strength, the aircrews awaited the assault on England with confidence and some impatience, although the magnitude of the task ahead must have been obvious. In particular, the Bf109 pilots realized that having to face a substantial number of Spitfires would tax their flying skill to the limit, and they had little enthusiasm for air combat over the Channel. There was a psychological, but very real, fear of dogfighting in a single-engined aircraft over water, where a damaged machine stood only a slim chance of getting home. A wounded pilot would be even less likely to survive if forced to ditch, even with an efficient air-sea rescue service looking for him. It was also easy to work out just how much time there would be for combat over England, given the Bf109's limited endurance—fifteen minutes on average, twenty at most.

Individual fighter pilots had seen what Spitfires and Hurricanes could do to Ju87s, making the already difficult job of protecting them almost impossible. Losses among the *Kampfgeschwader* had also been relatively high considering the quality of

the fighter opposition encountered thus far, and escorting the Dorniers, Heinkels and Junkers would be equally exacting—although just how much their own operations would be curtailed by escort duty was little realized at the outset of the Battle of Britain. These known drawbacks were compounded by limited knowledge of the numbers of British fighters and the extent of radar coverage in the main target areas.

Notwithstanding the difficulties, of all branches of the Luftwaffe committed to the air operations before *Seelöwe*, the *Jagdflieger* would acquit themselves best—indeed, there would be numerous occasions when the Bf109 was more than a match for anything put up by the RAF. Had the German fighter pilots been allowed to conduct operations the way they knew to be the most effective throughout the summer of 1940, subsequent events may have taken an entirely different turn.

Despite the German High Command having planned for an invasion of England well before the war, many details were still vaguely defined in 1940, although the primary objective was clear enough. Göring's directive on 30 June emphasized that it was 'to attack the enemy air force by day and night, in the air and on the ground, without consideration of other tasks'. In the event, outside pressures resulted in the Luftwaffe undertaking 'other tasks' to the degree that eventually the primary objective was overlooked. Well might the bomber leaders lament the lack of long-range four-engined aircraft, confronted as they were with a target list that ranged from aircraft factories to radar installations and power stations to shipping.

Two *Luftflotten* would be responsible for most of the sorties against England—Albert Kesselring's *Luftflotte* 2 in Holland, Belgium and north-eastern France and *Luftflotte* 3 under Hugo Sperrle, based in north-western France. Hans-Jurgen Stumpff's *Luftflotte* 5 in Scandinavia had only light forces available and would not take a significant part in the operation. Within each *Luftflotte*, the fighter and *Zerstörer* units were: *Luftflotte* 2: JG 3, JG 26, JG 51, JG 52, JG 54, ZG 26, ZG 76 and LG 2. *Luftflotte* 3: JG 2, JG 27, JG 53 and ZG 2. *Luftflotte* 5: I/ZG 76 and II/JG 77.

In the anti-shipping strikes that marked the opening stages of the Battle of Britain, there was the dual purpose of denying the Channel to the enemy and drawing the RAF into combat so that it could be destroyed before the proposed landing points were neutralized. Interception of such raids did cost the RAF a number of fighters to free chase formations of Bf109s that were always a danger; but in time, large formations of fighters came to be recognized as the bait they were.

Bad weather reduced combat early in July, although Bf109s engaged on a number of occasions and shot down three Hurricanes on the 4th. The German fighters were also kept busy intercepting RAF reconnaissance flights over the Continent. On 5 July machines of JG 51 caught three Spitfires at 22,000 ft over the Pas de Calais, shot one down and damaged another, with one Bf109 taking hits. Although RAF squadron aircraft soon discontinued such flights, specially modified Spitfires were a constant irritation and challenge to the Luftwaffe fighter pilots. Their heavy losses at this time (seven in a week) caused fighter escort to be requested for the regular reconnaissance flights by German bombers over the Channel area. On the 9th *Zerstörers* made their first sorties in strength; some sixty Bf110s and 109s provided cover for bombers bound for a convoy forming up in the mouth of the Thames. In the heaviest air fighting to date, three Bf110s and two Bf109s were shot down by intercepting fighters. It became regular practice for the Bf110s to form an *Abwehrkreis* ('death circle') when attacked, each aircraft entering a continuous turn over a fixed point, each covering the tail of the machine in front. The manoeuvre did not prevent individual Bf110s from being picked off, however.

Throughout the Battle of Britain, the RAF sent bombers to targets in Germany and the occupied territories, and on 9 July No. 82 Sqn. mounted a 12-Blenheim attack on *Luftflotte* 5's main base at Stavanger. Having dropped its bombs, the formation ran into three Bf110s of I/ZG 76 and three *Staffeln* of JG 77's Bf109s. Seven Blenheims went down and none of the survivors escaped damage.

For German pilots flying the average two or three sorties daily over the Channel, the physical strain

Major, fighter branch, summer 1940, wearing the optional white summer uniform for officers. This young Geschwader commander or staff officer, sporting the Spanish Cross on the right breast, wears the pin-on Iron Cross 1st Class and the ribbon of the 2nd Class. His pilot/observer qualification badge and a black (3rd Class) wound badge appear on the left breast. The white uniform bore a silver pin-on breast eagle rather than an embroidered wire one; note also lack of silver collar piping. Collar patches and epaulettes of rank are conventional, with the yellow backing of the flying branch. The silver-grey on blue cuff-title on the right sleeve bears the honour-title of his unit.

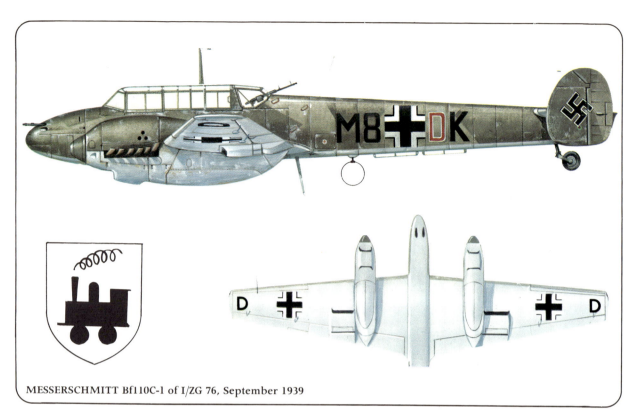

MESSERSCHMITT Bf110C-1 of I/ZG 76, September 1939

MESSERSCHMITT Bf109E-3 of 3/JG 51, winter 1939

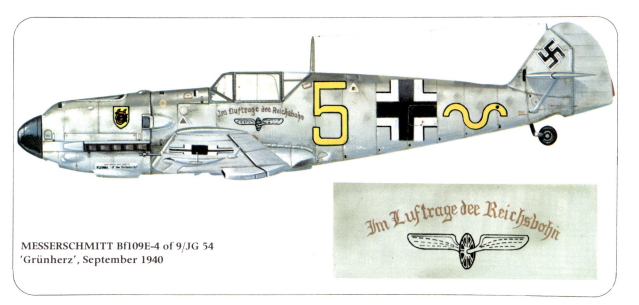

MESSERSCHMITT Bf109E-4 of 9/JG 54
'Grünherz', September 1940

Im Luftrage dee Reichsbahn

OPPOSITE, TOP: Messerschmitt Bf110C-1 of 2 Staffel, I Gruppe, Zerstörergeschwader 76, as it appeared during the Polish campaign of September 1939. The machine is finished in standard factory camouflage for this type; a splinter pattern of RLM shades 70 and 71 over all upper and side surfaces and an overall coat of pale blue shade 65 on the lower surfaces. National insignia are conventional. On the fuselage sides appear the Geschwader code 'M8' (always to the left of the cross) followed by the individual aircraft code 'D' and the Staffel code 'K'. The aircraft letter is in red trimmed with white, the colour coding for the second Staffel in each Gruppe. It is repeated in black under the wingtips; sometimes, but not invariably, it was also repeated above the wingtips in white. The detail view illustrates the 'Locomotivstaffel' emblem adopted by 1/ZG 76 as a result of their train-strafing operations in Poland; aircraft of the first Staffel were finished in the same scheme as those of the second, but bore the final code letter 'H' instead of 'K'. The emblem was painted on the port side of the nose beneath the windscreen.

OPPOSITE, BOTTOM: Messerschmitt Bf109E-3 of 3 Staffel, I Gruppe, Jagdgeschwader 51, as it appeared during the winter of 1939/40. The splinter camouflage scheme of shades 70 and 71 extends over the entire top and side surfaces and pale blue 65 is limited to the under surfaces and the tail struts. The very large national insignia on the wing upper surfaces are interesting, as is the swastika tail insignia placed across the hinge-line of fin and rudder. Note the yellow octane triangle behind the cockpit, bearing a black stencilled '87'. The '3' is the individual aircraft identification number, painted in the yellow which identified the third Staffel of each Gruppe. The absence of any emblem behind the fuselage cross identified the first Gruppe of each Geschwader. The chamois emblem is that of the Gruppe, I/JG 51; the yellow hand is the emblem of the Staffel, 3/JG 51. The canopy framing is painted in shade 71, the lighter of the two green tones.

ABOVE: Messerschmitt Bf109E-4 flown by Leutnant Waldemar ('Hein') Wübke of 9 Staffel, III Gruppe, Jagdgeschwader 54 'Grünherz', from Guines in the Pas-de-Calais region of France in September 1940. This interesting scheme is typical, in general distribution of colours, of the later stages of the Battle of Britain. The official factory scheme now involved the limiting of the splinter camouflage to the fuselage spine and the wing and tail upper surfaces, the blue 65 being brought up to a hard line level with the cockpit. At unit level a mottled overspray of shades of green and grey was often added along the fuselage sides and on the vertical tail surface. In the case of this aircraft, the splinter camouflage is—unusually—in shades 71 and 02 rather than 70 and 71; and the mottling is in shade 02.

The '5' is the individual aircraft code, in the yellow of the third Staffel of the Gruppe, usually trimmed with black on the pale blue background. The yellow emblem aft of the fuselage cross is that of the third Gruppe in the Geschwader. The devil insignia on the nose is that of the Staffel, 9/JG 54. The emblem below the cockpit, on the port side only, is a personal decoration. It features the badge of the German railway service and a legend which roughly translates as 'In the aerial service of the State Railways'. This is not, as might appear, a presentation inscription recording fund-raising by loyal railwaymen, but rather a bitter jest on the part of the pilot. It records the frustration of the single-seat fighter pilots at the orders from Göring which kept them on close bomber escort work—'driving trains'—instead of using their full combat potential in free-chase fighter combat.

MESSERSCHMITT Bf109E-1 of Staffelkapitän, 2/JG 27, early 1940

PAGES 28–29: Messerschmitt Bf109E-1 flown by Ober-leutnant G. Framm as Staffelkapitän of 2 Staffel, I Gruppe, Jagdgeschwader 27 early in 1940. The splinter camouflage is conventional, but appears from photographic evidence to have been in shades 71 and 02. National insignia are also conventional for the period—note that the upper wing crosses are now much slimmer and smaller than those illustrated at the foot of p. 26. The white-trimmed red markings and the red pennant and spinner refer to the second Staffel of the Gruppe, always identified in red. The number '1' was normally carried by Staffel commanders at this stage of the war, but the practice rapidly became unpopular when serious opposition was encountered in 1940—it obviously singled out the commander for the attentions of the enemy. The rear fuselage band is also a command insignia, but an unusual and possibly unique one. The tin pennant on the radio mast was another marking which did not long survive the opening of hostilities. The name SAMOA on the port side of the cowling was one of a sequence used in this Staffel since the days of the first commander of the Gruppe, Hauptmann Helmut Riegel: each machine carried the name of a former German colony.

BELOW: Messerschmitt Bf110C-3 of 3 Staffel, I Gruppe, Zerstörergeschwader 2, which was based on the Amiens airfield complex in September 1940. The splinter camouflage scheme is in shades 70 and 71, with pale blue 65 undersides. The yellow spinner tips and

individual code letter refer to the third Staffel in the Gruppe, as does the final 'L'. Note the areas of overpainting with shade 02 on the fuselage and 65 beneath the wingtips, where the original markings have been obscured. This machine served initially with I/ZG 52, whose code was 'A2' and whose insignia was the dragon emblem illustrated here. This Gruppe was disbanded and its aircraft incorporated into ZG 2, but examples with the original insignia were still to be seen after the re-designation, particularly in the II Gruppe of ZG 2 where the 'A2' fuselage code persisted for some time.

OPPOSITE, TOP: Examples of fighter unit emblems: (1) I/JG 54 'Grünherz' (2) Stab/JG 1 (3) ZG 26 'Horst Wessel' (4) 9/JG 2 'Richthofen' (5) Stab, III/JG 26 'Schlageter'.

OPPOSITE, BOTTOM: Kfz 12 (Mercedes Benz 230) 4 × 2 field car, as used by 9 Staffel, JG 26 'Schlageter' as a general purpose vehicle around the Pas-de-Calais airfields in the autumn of 1940. This illustration is prepared from a photograph which shows the Staffel emblem painted on the car in solid white silhouette; the style in which it was normally marked on the unit's aircraft is shown in the detail view. The vehicle is finished in dark blue-grey, characteristic of Luftwaffe vehicles; the number plate would begin with the letters 'LW-' followed by a five or six digit number, in black on white.

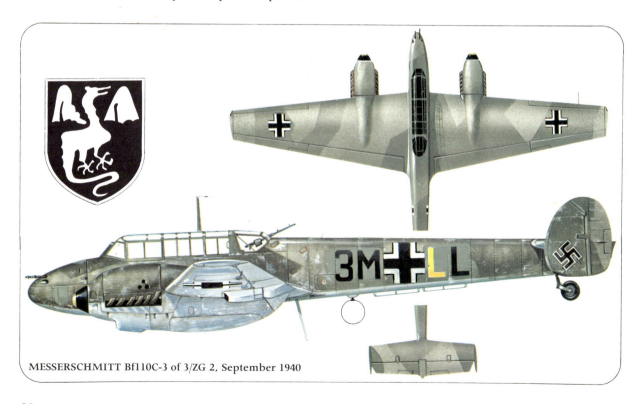

MESSERSCHMITT Bf110C-3 of 3/ZG 2, September 1940

1

2

3

4

5

MERCEDES BENZ 230 (Kfz 12) field car, 9/JG 26
'Schlageter', autumn 1940

Unteroffizier of ground crew, 1940–41. This senior NCO wears the regulation Luftwaffe other ranks' sidecap or 'Schiff', with working overalls and regulation leather belt. The overalls appeared in both one- and two-piece versions, in dark blue-grey and black. Pre-war overalls often had two breast pockets, but from 1938 a single right pocket was normal—though some overalls lacked both. Insignia was limited to silver NCO 'Tresse' round the collar for the rank of Unteroffizier, and silver sleeve stripes for higher ranks: one for a Feldwebel, two for Oberfeldwebel, three for Hauptfeldwebel, and three over a star for Stabsfeldwebel.

Fighter pilot, summer 1940, in casual flying clothing. Over his service dress shirt and breeches this young officer pilot wears the fighter-style life jacket, regulation black flying boots with suede legs and leather uppers complete with a rubber 'bandolier' of flare pistol cartridges, and the lightweight summer flying helmet. This latter has a 'netting' skull and leather headband and earpieces. The only insignia worn with this uniform would be the slip-on uniform epaulettes worn on the shirt, obscured here by the life jacket.

was considerable. Even for a man of average height and build, the cockpit of the Bf109 was cramped and the heavy canopy framing necessitated constant head movements in order to spot enemy aircraft. Space was further limited by the extra equipment which was carried, in case the pilot had to put down in the Channel. To help rescue-craft locate him, he had cartridges for a Mauser flare pistol strapped around the top of each flying boot; the pistol itself was attached to the life jacket. An inflatable life-raft was also stowed in the cockpit.

There was no radio or radar guidance from the ground and although Messerschmitt pilots could talk to each other in the air via their radio telephones, they could not contact bomber formations. The R/T sets were often unreliable and a man had to have a keen sense of sight if he was to survive. If he came under attack, there was an 8 mm armour-plate panel above his head and 10 mm armoured bulkheads at each side of the cockpit to protect him. Towards the end of the Battle of

31. Close-up of an 'Emil' of JG 53 'Pik As' which shows to advantage the back and head armour fitted to the canopy of later marks. Comparison of tones suggests that the cowling is yellow and the partly visible code number is white; the machine presumably flew with 7 Staffel, if this is so. (Bildarchiv)

Britain, some Bf109s were fitted with an external bullet-proof windscreen of 56 mm thick armour glass.

For sighting his target, the pilot had a Revi C/12C reflector gunsight; the weight of fire of the two wing-mounted cannon and twin fuselage machine guns of the Bf109E was equal to that of most contemporary fighters of the period and, in killing power, better than most. The cannon fired high explosive, armour-piercing incendiary ammunition at the rate of 520 rpm and the machine guns at 1,100 rpm. A thumb button on the control column fired the wing guns, a finger trigger the fuselage weapons.

Although his aircraft was far less potent than the

Bf109, the Bf110 pilot did at least have a roomier cockpit and a wireless operator/gunner to share the workload on each sortie and he could bring to bear a very heavy weight of fire from his closely-grouped nose guns—when his machine could out-manoeuvre its opponent. Sluggish in comparison with the Spitfire and Hurricane, the early Bf110Cs also lacked armour protection for the crew or the fuel tanks, hence their use of the *Abwehrkreis* to give each other some mutual cover in combat.

With the hated *'Scheisskanal'* proving almost as great a hazard to the Luftwaffe as was the RAF, every effort was made to rescue downed aircrew. Early in the Battle of Britain, Heinkel He59 floatplanes and Do18 flying boats operated independent searches, but fighter escort became necessary when those same machines were suspected of radioing convoy positions and became legitimate RAF targets.

The build-up to the large-scale raids of August and September continued in July, convoys remaining the principal Luftwaffe targets. On the 13th the first major operation was flown by the Bf110s of V/LG 1. Failing to find their target convoy, the forty aircraft formed a defensive circle as Hurricanes intercepted and, on this occasion, it proved impregnable; only three Bf110s were damaged.

A Führer Directive issued on the 16th confirmed the Germans' intention of invading England, and areas of operation were allocated to each *Luftflotte* to pave the way. Fortunately for the defenders, much of the accompanying target information was out of date, and there tended to be an optimistic view of the capabilities of available Luftwaffe bombers to reach them. By the 18th, preparations to implement *Seelöwe* were complete; assembly of barges was started and more Luftwaffe units became operational in France and the Low Countries.

Though heavy rain restricted Luftwaffe sorties, and turned some French airfields into quagmires, the *Jagdflieger* who managed to take off surprised Spitfires of 610 Sqn. by forming up over France and circling like a bomber formation, specially for the benefit of the radar controllers across the Channel. One Spitfire was shot down.

On 19 July, JG 2 scored a considerable success when II *Gruppe* executed a carefully planned attack on Defiants of No. 141 Sqn. Recognizing the turret fighters for what they were, the Bf109s bored in from below and astern and inflicted heavy losses. A second *Staffel* attack from below and ahead completed the decimation of the British formation; RAF figures confirmed that seven Defiants had been shot down or severely damaged. Though the Defiants' days as front-line fighters were numbered by the events of that day, they did appear once or twice more. Two days later, the Bf110Cs of V/LG 1 made their debut in the fighter-bomber role, carrying out a dive attack on a convoy which was passing south of the Needles. One aircraft was damaged by a Hurricane and had to crash-land at Theville, killing one of the crew.

JG 26 and JG 52 mounted both free-chase and escort sorties on 24 July, individual aircraft having to break off combat and streak for home at the baleful red glow of the fuel warning light. *Ltn.* Heinrich Bartels of III/JG 26 was wounded in a dogfight with Spitfires. Four days later, Werner Mölders was caught by No. 74 Sqn. off Dover. Four *Staffeln* from I and II/JG 51 were escorting bombers as the Spitfires joined combat. One Bf109 of 6/JG 51 fell to 'Sailor' Malan's guns. *Oblt.* R. Leppla of 3/JG 51 claimed to have shot down the Spitfire that hit Mölders' machine, but it is unclear which Spitfire this was.

On 29 July the Bf110Cs of *Erprobungsgruppe* (*Erpr.*) 210 based at St Omer came to grips with Hurricanes, their targets being the port of Dover and Channel shipping. The combat was inconclusive: only one German and two British aircraft were damaged and Dover was left almost unscathed.

August was a month of intense air activity, with heavy raids in mid-month; both sides were feeling the strain of constant combat flying, but the Luftwaffe was soon to come very near to achieving its primary aim. Non-operational attrition took its toll on the 7th when 3/*Erpr.* 210's *Staffelkapitän*, *Hptm.* Valesi crashed in a Bf109E-4. Valesi was one of the Luftwaffe's most experienced exponents of fighter-bomber tactics and his loss was a shock, especially as the cause of the accident was never discovered.

There was hectic activity over the Channel in the second week of August, when waves of Bf109s and Bf110s covered the Ju87s of *Fliegerkorps* VIII. A maximum effort on the 8th brought air combat on such a scale that this was long regarded as the opening of the Battle of Britain. In two strikes against a convoy, the *Jagdflieger* became heavily engaged with RAF fighters which accounted for twelve of the *Stukas* as well as the *Gruppenkommandeur* of II/JG 27, *Maj.* Werner Andres, who became a prisoner. In five weeks of operations, the Luftwaffe had lost 106 Bf109s and 110s, while Fighter Command lost 148 Hurricanes, Spitfires and Defiants.

Thundery squalls limited action during the following few days, although 10 August was originally scheduled as the start of *Adlerangriff*, Göring's 'Attack of the Eagles'. There were considerable fighter losses on the 11th, including the *Staffelkapitän* of I/ZG 26 (*Hptm.* Kogler) and of II/JG 2 (*Oblt.* Rempel). The former was captured but the latter was killed when his Bf109E-4 crashed into the sea. Casualties among the Bf110 formations were high: seventeen aircraft lost, eleven from ZG 2.

As a prelude to *Adlerangriff*, attacks were made on the British coastal radar chain on 12 August, *Erpr.*210's well executed series of strikes putting the stations at Dover, Pevensey and Rye temporarily out of action. Ventnor radar was off the air for three hours after a dive-bombing attack by KG 51's Ju88s, but ten machines did not return when top cover Bf109s failed to come to their aid in time when British fighters intercepted. Free-chase sorties were also flown by Bf109s.

Adlerangriff was finally launched in mid-afternoon of 13 August, raids being directed at No. 12 Group airfields and Southampton docks. *Stukas* devastated Detling, but the airfield was not a vital sector station. Another Ju87 formation, heading for Middle Wallop, was intercepted and cut to pieces by Spitfires of No. 609 Sqn., the Bf109 escort having had to turn for home because they were low on fuel. The carnage among the *Stukageschwader* was nearly at an end, losses having become prohibitive—the skies of southern England were no place for the slow dive-bombers.

Equally, Bristol Blenheims could not expect to escape lightly when Bf109s were about. On the 13th, eleven Blenheims of No. 82 Sqn. struck JG 77's base at Aalborg in Norway; six of them fell to pilots of 6 *Staffel*, helped by the ever-efficient flak.

The most disastrous single day for the *Zerstörers* was 15 August, when twenty-six Bf110s were destroyed, including aircraft from I/ZG 76 in *Luftflotte* 5; more than 200 Bf110s would go down before the campaign was terminated. Four days later, Göring berated the fighter pilots for failing to achieve the desired air superiority over south-east England. He refused to accept that faulty planning was the chief cause of this 'failure', and his own blind faith in the *Zerstörers* could not be shaken, despite their losses. The answer, as the *Reichsmarshall* read the situation, was to reshuffle the command structure of the *Jagdflieger*, with the result that several *Kommodore* were removed and younger men, considered more aggressive, filled their places. But even gifted pilots like Galland, Trautloft and Lutzow could not work miracles; their own remedy, more independent fighter sweeps, did not move Göring. He did allow commanders more leeway in choosing their own targets, but ordered the Bf109s to escort the heavy fighters, restricting the flexibility of the single-seaters even more and denying them the very tactics that were the biggest threat to the RAF.

Night raids were now increasing in intensity and in an effort to deny the defence any respite by day, there were many small-scale strikes by the Luftwaffe. Big attacks were renewed on the 24/25th, when scores of *Zerstörers* escorted bombers, excluding Ju87s—Göring having effectively removed these from any further large-scale participation in the battle. Defiants were in action again on the 24th and 26th; the latter day brought a swift victory for the Bf109s when 30 of them jumped No. 616 Sqn., bringing down seven Spitfires in less than 30 seconds. Defiants of No. 264 Sqn. successfully drew the Bf109s away from a Dornier formation so that Hurricanes could attack.

Few Luftwaffe pilots enjoyed even 24 hours' leave during those dramatic months of 1940,

although a commanding officer would grant rest periods at his own discretion, but individual commanders were severely criticized for regular rotation of operational pilots, even when the latter were on the point of extreme fatigue.

Late August saw a concentrated effort to destroy Fighter Command; the full weight of Kesselring's *Luftflotte* 2, boosted by most of the Bf109 *Gruppen* of *Luftflotte* 3, was thrown against No. 11 Group airfields in south-east England. On the 28th, no less than seven *Gruppen* of Bf109s from JG 2, 3, 26, 27, 51, 54 and *Erpr.* 210 were in action, most of which suffered heavy losses, but they succeeded in keeping bomber casualties down.

The night offensive against London was building up by the end of August, when a spell of good weather heralded the climax of the Battle of Britain—a climax in which the Luftwaffe, while taking a heavy toll of British fighters, was to throw away the chance of beating Fighter Command. The RAF was avoiding combat with the vast formations of Bf109s, and Kesselring dispatched his bombers in waves; on 30 August, no less than nineteen *Gruppen* penetrated into Kent and the Thames Estuary in two hours. Hundreds of Luftwaffe sorties were flown during the spell of fine weather. Raids on Biggin Hill early on the 31st were interspersed with hit-and-run strikes by *Erpr.* 210 on radar sites in Kent and Sussex. Switching its role later in the day, the unit was back over England at 17.30, shielding Ju88s and bomb-carrying Bf110s intent on destruction at Biggin Hill and Hornchurch. LG 1 was also in combat, five of its Bf110s and two Ju88s failing to return. The ever-present danger of collision when forming up a large number of aircraft became reality for two Bf109s of 3/JG 51, both pilots bailing out over Calais.

The heavy day raids continued in early September; on the 2nd, 160 Bf109s caught eighty-five Hurricanes and Spitfires in a classic fighter trap. Breaking away and climbing the Bf109s led the Hurricanes into the evening sun where another *Staffel* was waiting. One Hurricane went down before the Dover AA guns joined in the mêlée.

Although the Luftwaffe's aircraft replacement was generally keeping pace with losses, the

experienced *Staffel* and *Gruppe* leaders, whose fate in many instances was unknown, were sorely missed. On 4 September *Erpr.* 210's *Kommandeur*, *Hptm.* von Boltenstern, was reported missing among nineteen fighters lost.

Some operational changes were made by the Luftwaffe at this time, on the one hand to give the fighters more flexibility and on the other to harry the defences even further. The *Jagdflieger*, desperate for more room to manoeuvre on close escort sorties, flew with greater separation between their formations and those of the bombers, but still keeping a *Staffel* above 20,000 ft. The RAF maxim to new pilots to 'beware the Hun in the sun' could not be overstressed. For their part, the *Kampfgeschwader* tried numerous attacks on 5 September by small formations on a wide selection of targets. On the 6th the *Gruppenkommandeur* of III/JG 27 was shot down by a Hurricane.

On 7 September Göring and his retinue watched, on the coast at the Pas de Calais, as nearly 1,000 aircraft, the strength of five *Kampfgeschwader*, seven *Jagdgeschwader* and a number of *Zerstörers* headed for the Thames estuary, their target: London. In this and over fifty subsequent raids, widespread loss of life and destruction was caused in the capital and its suburbs, but the *Reichsmarshall* had made his biggest tactical blunder of the Battle of Britain: in attacking London, he spared the remnants of Fighter Command.

The second week in September brought a lull in the day fighting. On the 14th, *Oblt.* Joachim Müncheberg, *Staffelkapitän* of 7/JG 26 scored his 20th victory and was awarded the Knight's Cross in accordance with the 1940 requirements for this much sought-after decoration—20 kills in air combat. Between May 1940 and May 1941, thirty-five fighter and six *Zerstörer* pilots received the award, but twenty victories did not automatically mean that a pilot was decorated. Whenever a claim was made, very careful checking was necessary before the award was authorized.

32. Bf110C about to take off in September 1940. After the Battle of Britain the type was never again taken seriously as a day fighter, and was relegated to fighter-bomber and night-fighter duties. (Bildarchiv)

Hitler still withheld a definite date for Operation *Seelöwe,* and 15 September showed him why he could never hope to succeed in that particular venture; on that day two massive raids were routed by strong formations of Spitfires and Hurricanes. The fighter pilots' escort task became impossible as the bombers broke formation under the onslaught and their own losses included the Bf109s flown by the *Staffelkapitäne* of 2/JG 3 and 3/JG 53.

Fighters flew a large number of sorties late in September in a belated attempt to renew the attack on Fighter Command's installations and aircraft supply centres. But it was too late; the RAF had taken advantage of the respite and fighter defence had improved considerably in the light of the experience of the last few months. On the 30th, the *Jagdflieger* lost twenty-eight Bf109s, the worst day for the single-seaters during the battle.

Fighter sorties continued as September drew to a close and there was a considerable number of strikes by fighter-bomber Bf109s in October, but, for the Germans, the worst part of a difficult task was over. They had not been defeated, but had been unable to achieve the victory demanded, and it is doubtful whether any such force could have, given the prevailing conditions. Many of its most able commanders were dead, incapacitated or prisoners; these were men of experience who would be hard to replace in the bitter campaigns that lay ahead. The pilots could be proud of having taken on—and in many instances beaten—men equal in skill to themselves, flying aircraft more than a match for their superb Emils. Those who came through the Battle of Britain knew that the kill markings which decorated the rudders of their machines had been hard won, but the price of 610 Bf109s and 235 Bf110s was high, for little more than experience.

Among the statistics of the battle were those showing the actual losses incurred by each side when the three principal single-seat fighters were in combat with each other. Thus, Spitfire *v.* Bf109: 219 to 180 lost; Hurricane *v.* Bf109: 272 to 153 lost—491 Spitfires and Hurricanes against 333 Bf109s was a ratio impressive enough to show just how effective the Luftwaffe's single-seaters were.

To cap the sobering events of the summer,

November brought the loss of one of the fighter arm's most gifted fighter leaders. On the 28th aircraft of JG 2 became involved in combat with Spitfires of No. 609 Sqn. Among the losses on the German side was the machine of *Maj.* Helmut Wick, *Kommodore* of the wing. One of only three pilots to be awarded the Oak Leaves to the Knight's Cross, Wick had at that time fifty-six victories to his credit at the age of twenty-two.

THE BALKANS

With the offensive against the British Isles almost exclusively in the hands of the night bombers, the majority of the *Jagdverbande* returned home to rest and re-equip with the last sub-types of the Bf109E pending the introduction of the Bf109F. The losses sustained over England led to most of the *Zerstörergruppen* being assigned other roles, the Bf110 becoming the mainstay of the night-fighter arm. Those Bf110 day-fighter formations that remained in being were to see most action in the Mediterranean area, III/ZG 26 being one of the first units to arrive in North Africa on 30 January 1941.

The Bf109 *Gruppen* remaining in France were to see only limited combat for some months, placed as they were in a situation very similar to that of RAF Fighter Command the previous summer. On 10 January, the RAF mounted the first *Circus* raid of the year when over 100 Spitfires and Hurricanes escorted Blenheims of No. 114 Sqn. in an attack on St Ingelvert airfield. *Circus* operations were designed primarily to tempt the Luftwaffe to battle, the Blenheims being little more than 'fighter bait'. But just as the Luftwaffe had found that the range of the Bf109E was critical in operations over England, so the endurance of the Spitfire and Hurricane was to limit the effectiveness of the early RAF penetrations of Europe—and success depended on the Germans being drawn into combat.

The 10 January raid achieved only the destruction of a single Bf109 by a Hurricane and some damage to the target. Bad weather curtailed *Circus* operations for three weeks, and the second raid did not take

place until 2 February when the target was Boulogne. In seven such attacks before the end of June, the RAF raided five airfields—three in the St Omer area and those at Calais-Marck and Desvres—and incurred some losses. Generally, however, there was only limited air combat on the Channel coast, the Luftwaffe fighters not being tempted to take on the superior formations of British fighters, against which they would have been sorely pressed.

The bulk of the German fighter force's combat operations were flown elsewhere in the first six months of 1941, as the Nazi sphere of influence spread further east. With the war becoming increasingly global, it was inevitable that the resources of both sides should be thinly stretched in certain areas—and some of those areas were about to become strategically vital to the Allies as Germany prepared to secure her territorial flanks for Operation *Barbarossa*.

Under the code name Operation *Marita,* the assault on the Balkans began at 05.15 hours on 6 April 1941 with German troops sweeping across the

33, 34. These photos are believed to show an NCO pilot named Nocker, serving with I/JG 1 at De Kooy, Holland, in the spring of 1941. Note the white rudder and wing-tips; other photos from the sequence show white cowlings as well. In the close-up the pilot is pointing out an enemy bullet-hole patched and marked with the nationality of the enemy responsible—a survival of a World War I custom. Surprisingly, for this date, the old kapok life-jacket is still worn, with a Mauser flare pistol strapped to it; the inflatable life-jacket had been in use in single-seat fighter units during the summer of 1940. Note the two victory bars, with RAF roundels indicating nationality. (Obert)

frontiers of Greece while German, Italian and Bulgarian forces attacked Yugoslavia. Rumania, with her vast oil complex at Ploesti which was invaluable to Germany, stayed loyal to her Axis pact. German ground forces based in Bulgaria moved south into Macedonia and west into Yugoslavia, supported by some 1,200 aircraft of *Luftflotte 4* under Alexander Löhr. The fighter units taking part in the campaign were: JG 27, JG 77 and LG 2 flying Bf109Es and the *Stab*, I and II *Gruppen* of ZG 26, with Bf110s. These machines generally retained their Channel Front markings, but because there were a number of German types in the inventories of the opposing air forces (including Do17s, Bf109s and Hs126s), the engine cowlings and rudders of the majority of them were prominently marked in yellow as an aid to recognition.

35. Bf109Es lined up in almost Staffel strength, bearing the markings of II Gruppe of an unidentified Jagdgeschwader. Two appear to be fitted with old-fashioned semi-external telescope gunsights passing through the windscreen, similar to the device favoured by the legendary Adolf Galland. (Bildarchiv)

Flying from bases in Bulgaria and Rumania, the Luftwaffe again found weak opposition in the air. Only a handful of the 154 Yugoslav fighters managed to get airborne; the 6th Fighter Regiment equipped with the Bf109E was the first to clash with Luftwaffe 'Emils'. Some air combat took place, but most of the Yugoslav air force was wiped out on the ground. Belgrade was heavily bombed on the 6th.

Tactical operations over Greece were hampered by bad weather, which lasted a week, but despite the conditions RAF ground attacks were pressed home and in combat with No. 33 Sqn. Hurricanes, five out of thirty Bf109s were shot down. British fighter strength in Greece was also limited, there being two Hurricane and one Blenheim fighter squadrons, plus a Gladiator unit.

By 9 April German and Italian forces had linked up in Albania, sealing the fate of Yugoslavia. In Greece German units reached Salonika and thus sealed off all of the eastern part of the country. On the 13th, six Blenheims of No. 211 Sqn. attacking German forces were jumped by Bf109s and all were shot down. The following day Hitler ordered the

complete occupation of Greece, as mopping-up continued in the initial target areas.

With the weather improving, the Luftwaffe was able to employ its full strength in support of the campaign. Fighters made strafing attacks on British airfields in the Lárisa plain on the 15th, effectively eliminating No. 113 Sqn.—all its Blenheims were destroyed or badly damaged. Two Hurricanes were also shot down and the RAF squadrons pulled back to the Athens area. An attack on Paramithia disabled forty-four aircraft of the Yugoslav air force, and a Greek Gladiator unit was wiped out on the 16th. Lárisa fell to the Germans on 19 April as the Luftwaffe turned its attention to the British air units remaining in the country.

Most Luftwaffe bombing raids were bitterly contested by British fighters and the air battle for Greece reached a peak on the 20th, when 100 Ju88s under heavy escort attacked Piraeus airfield. Strafing Bf110s of ZG 26 disabled a further twelve Blenheims, and five Hurricanes were lost in the day's air fighting, one of them flown by Sqn. Ldr. 'Pat' Pattle, the RAF's leading fighter ace, at the time, with forty-one victories. The Greeks suffered a major loss at the hands of Bf110s on 23 April when fourteen Hurricanes and a number of trainers were destroyed at Argos airfield. That afternoon, the remnants of the Greek Air Force and RAF were evacuated to Crete, the fight for Greece having cost the British seventy-two combat losses and the Germans 164.

The main evacuation of British forces to Crete began on the 24th and was completed on the 30th, three days after the Germans reached Athens. By occupying airfields on the Greek mainland, the Morea Peninsula, and the Greek and Dodecanese islands the Luftwaffe could effectively close the northern, western, and eastern approaches to Crete. To defend the island, some twenty RAF Hurricanes and Gladiators, and Fulmars of 805 Sqn. FAA were based at Máleme, Heraklion and Retimo—the critical situation in the Mediterranean meant that no more British aircraft could be spared.

An island some twenty miles wide and 150 miles long, Crete was the last bar to German control of the Aegean and Mediterranean coasts and Britain

36. Messerschmitt Bf110D-3s of I/ZG 26 (note wing-mounted 198 Imperial gallon drop-tanks) operating over Greece in summer 1941. (Bildarchiv)

resolved to hold it; this resolution was to cost the Germans dear. The plans for Operation *Mercury*, the German assault, were known to the defenders in advance and they were well prepared with the limited resources available. After feverish marshalling of forces, the German attack began on 20 May, four days later than planned.

From 06.00 hours, elements of *Gen.* Wolfram von Richthofen's *Fliegerkorps VIII* pounded the village of Máleme, with its airfield and strategic terrain. Bf109s of JG 77 and Bf110s of ZG 26 came streaking in over the sea to shoot up anti-aircraft and infantry positions before the first wave of gliders appeared overhead.

One of the major problems confronting the Luftwaffe was the condition of the Greek airfields that had to be used for the Crete operation. Most were little more than flat desert strips and every take-off created a dense cloud of dust that effectively halted following aircraft until it had settled. Water wagons were used to spray each airfield in an effort to lay the blinding dust, but it remained a hazard.

There was precious little opposition for the *Jagdflieger* sorties over Crete, but on 14 May six Bf109s were shot down, one to ground fire. Two Hurricanes were destroyed in air combat, while a

37, 38. The Bf109E-7s of the 'Red Heart Staffel'—7/JG 26 'Schlageter'—led a nomadic existence in 1941, being sent south to Sicily in February, and later to Africa and Greece. These photos illustrate the Staffel emblem on the nose, and in the more distant shot the S-shield of the Geschwader emblem can be seen below the windscreen. The white fuselage band indicates service in the Southern theatre of operations. The machine beside which the unidentified officer is practising equitation bears the vertical bar behind the cross which replaced the 'squiggle' as the III Gruppe symbol in 1941. (US National Archives)

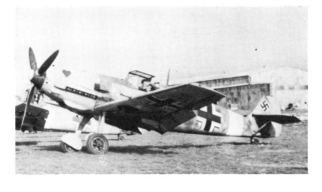

Hurricane and the last of the Fulmars were smashed on the ground. By the 19th the remaining fighters, four Hurricanes and three Gladiators, departed for Egypt, from whence all further Allied air support was mounted. There was thus no enemy air opposition to the Germans left on Crete.

There was, however, the threat of the Royal Navy. To support their troops fighting hard for control of Crete, the Germans had to employ commandeered Greek caiques and small coasters. RN units sank a number of caiques making their way to the island on the night of 21/22 May; and at first light on 22 May, airfields in the Dodecanese reverberated to the roar of engines as the Luftwaffe prepared to close the approaches to the enemy fleet. Dive and conventional bombers were supported by the Bf109Es of I (Jagd)/LG 2 on the island of Molae, then operating as the third *Gruppe* of JG 77, the *Stab*, II and III *Gruppen* of which shared the airfield.

The *Stab*, I and II *Gruppen* of ZG 26 had meanwhile occupied Argos.

The bombers damaged a number of British cruisers and destroyers in the morning strikes, and soon after noon the battleship *Warspite* came under attack from a *Schwarm* of Bf109 fighter bombers of I (Jagd) LG 2 under Wolf-Dietrich Huy. Approaching the ship head-on, the four Messerschmitts used their bombs with telling effect, wrecking *Warspite*'s 4 in and 6 in gun batteries. Repeated sorties by bombers and *Stukas*, ably supported by ZG 26's Bf110s and the Bf109s of JG 77, gave the British fleet a hard time, the ships having no air cover. Such was the Luftwaffe's domination of the skies over Crete that small groups of bombers were able to take off as soon as their fuel tanks and bomb racks were replenished, there being little need to wait for a fighter escort.

At 17.45 hours the cruiser *Fiji*, making her way to Alexandria with a destroyer screen, was spotted by a lone Bf109 of I/LG 2 which was about to return to base, having reached the limit of its endurance. The pilot nevertheless elected to attack and placed his 500 lb bomb squarely against the ship's side, where its mine-like effect tore a large hole. Dead in the water, *Fiji* took on a heavy list. The Messerschmitt

39. This is probably a machine of SKG 210 photographed during the first winter of the Russian campaign, and it thus falls outside the scope of this book; but the ventral ETC-50 bomb-rack beneath the fuselage, carrying four 50 kg bombs, is the same equipment as was used by 'Jabos' on the Channel coast in 1941.

pilot summoned a second *Jabo* by radio, which arrived on the scene some thirty minutes later. This time the bomb exploded in the forward boiler room and, at 19.17, *Fiji* capsized.

By 17 May it was clear that Crete could not be held; the following night Allied troops began to be taken off and, by 2 June, some 16,000 men had been evacuated. The cost of the operation was high and although the Germans secured the island, the cream of the elite paratroop force had been wiped out; no further operations of this kind were carried out. More serious was the time the operation had taken, putting the invasion of Russia back by one month—perhaps a vital one.

Throughout the Balkans operation the Luftwaffe had played its part with characteristic thoroughness, being instrumental in the destruction of two air forces, a considerable number of troops and equipment and the sinking of two RN cruisers and four destroyers and damage to others.

43

NEW FIGHTERS

With the Mediterranean war occupying many of their comrades, the fighter pilots left on the Channel Front were the first to receive examples of the Bf109F. Having had its rear fuselage strengthened after a number of failures due to the introduction of an unbraced tailplane, the Bf109F-1 was delivered to III/JG 26 and JG 2 in March, and it began to replace the Bf109E in JG 51 and JG 53 the following month; by the time of *Barbarossa*, all but seven *Gruppen* of the fighter arm in eastern Europe were equipped with it.

Although the Bf109F was generally considered to be an improvement over the Bf109E, particularly in rate of climb and turning radius, there was considerable criticism of its armament from pilots, mainly because there were no wing guns. The Bf109F had a centrally-mounted 20 mm MG FF cannon firing through the spinner and two 7.9 mm machine guns above the cowling, which gave a fine concentration of fire, but meant that a pilot's aim had to be that much more accurate. Adolf Galland, then *Kommodore* of JG 26, could see that the average squadron pilot needed a better spread of fire in order to hit his target, and only wing guns could achieve this. The question was partially resolved by fitting later Bf109Fs with underwing gondolas, each with an MG 151/20 cannon, but these installations were detrimental to the machine's manoeuvrability and were not popular with all pilots.

Early 1941 also saw the introduction of the Bf110E, able to carry four 110 lb bombs on wing racks in addition to a single 550 lb bomb under the fuselage centre-section. Bomb-carrying capability was further increased on the Bf110E-1/R2, which could accommodate two 2,200 lb bombs. Range was boosted by the addition of attachment points for two 198 imp gallon drop tanks on the Bf110E-3, the last variant of the E series to see service.

As the build-up for *Barbarossa* continued in the late spring and early summer, other war theatres were denuded of their operational *Gruppen*; by the middle of June, only JG 2 and JG 26 remained on the Channel coast, II/JG 26 still retaining its Bf109E-7s. To make up for the lack of bomber units in the West, there was an increase in *Jabo* operations against shipping and targets in the British Isles. More successful than earlier attempts to use the Bf109 in the fighter-bomber role the previous summer, the operations of early 1941 led to the formation of specialized units later in the year.

For the *Jagdflieger,* what began in the early hours of 22 April 1941 was to surpass anything they had yet experienced—the fastest victory rate ever achieved in the history of air warfare by one air force over another. Operation *Barbarossa* was to give the fighter pilots of the Luftwaffe a record of kills that will never be beaten.

MAJOR UNITS FROM SEPTEMBER 1939

Jagdgeschwader 1
Unit designation originated before the war; I *Gruppe* saw combat in Poland with Bf109Ds; became III/JG 27, 6 July 1940. Saw combat in France and based in Holland early 1941.

Lehrgeschwader 1
First operational development *Geschwader*. I (Z)/LG 1 one of the first three Luftwaffe *Gruppen* with Bf110; saw combat in Poland. V(Z)/LG 1 with Bf110 saw combat in Battle of Britain.

Zerstörergeschwader 1
Combat in Poland, I Gruppe with Bf110 and II with Bf109. I/ZG 1 operated in Norwegian campaign; II *Gruppe* became III/ZG 76 on 6 July, 1940. I *Gruppe* reformed as NJG 1, 20 July 1940.

Lehrgeschwader 2
Second operational development *Geschwader*; I (Jagd)/LG 2 saw combat in Poland with Bf109E; operated Bf109E-7 in fighter-bomber role and E-1 and E-4 on escort duty in the Battle of Britain; 7 Staffel equipped with Bf110C-5. Only I and II (*Schlacht*) saw combat in Battle of Britain. I(J)/LG 2 operated in Balkans April/May 1941.

Jagdgeschwader 2 'Richthofen'
Unit designation originated before the war; I Gruppe with Bf109E. 10 (*Nacht*)/JG 2 at Jever with Bf109C/D late 1939, and with 11 Staffel and 10 (*Nacht*)/JG 26, formed IV/JG 2, 2 February 1940. Brought up to three *Gruppen* strength by April 1940. Saw combat in France and Battle of Britain and remained in France, being one of first units to receive Bf109F in March 1941 (all *Gruppen*).

Zerstörergeschwader 2
I/ZG 2 only unit equipped with Bf109D for combat in

Poland. I and II *Gruppen* received Bf110s spring/summer 1940. IV(N)/ZG 2 became III/NJG 1 and I/ZG 52 became II/ZG 2, July 1940. I and II *Gruppen* saw combat in Battle of Britain.

Jagdgeschwader 3 'Udet'
Unit designation originated before the war; I Gruppe with Bf109E. Brought up to three *Gruppen* strength by April 1940. Saw combat in France and Battle of Britain.

Jagdgeschwader 21
I Gruppe saw combat in Poland with Bf109E/C, became III/JG 54, 6 July 1940. Fought in Battle of France.

Jagdgeschwader 26 'Schlageter'
Unit designation originated before the war; I Gruppe formed prior to September 1939. 10 (*Nacht*)/JG 26 at Jever with Bf109C, late 1939. Brought up to three *Gruppen* strength by April 1940. Saw combat in France and Battle of Britain and remained on Channel coast. Only I and III *Gruppen* had received Bf109F by June 1941.

Zerstörergeschwader 26 'Horst Wessel'
All three *Gruppen* equipped with Bf109 by outbreak of war; all had converted to Bf110 by summer 1940. All three *Gruppen* saw combat in France and Battle of Britain. III *Gruppe* to North Africa January 1941. I and II *Gruppe* operated in Balkans April/May 1941.

Jagdgeschwader 27 'Afrika'
I *Gruppe* formed 1 October 1939, II *Gruppe* 1 January 1940. Both *Gruppen* saw combat in France and unit brought up to three *Gruppen* strength for combat in Battle of Britain, I/JG 1 becoming III/JG 27 on 6 June 1940. I *Gruppe* to North Africa April 1941.

Jagdgeschwader 51
Unit designation originated before the war; I *Gruppe* on home defence duties September 1939. Second *Gruppe* added to strength by April 1940. I/JG 20 became III/JG 51, 6 April 1940. All three *Gruppen* saw combat in France and Battle of Britain.

Jagdgeschwader 52
Unit designation originated before the war. II *Gruppe* formed with Bf109Ds, September 1939. I *Gruppe* became II/ZG 2, 6 July 1940. Three *Gruppen* strength by April 1940 for combat in France and Battle of Britain. III *Gruppe* based in Rumania 1941.

Jagdgeschwader 53 'Pik As'
Unit designation originated before the war; home defence 1939. All three *Gruppen* saw combat in France and Battle of Britain.

Jagdgeschwader 54 'Grünherz'
III *Gruppe* formed from I/JG 21 late 1939; I *Gruppe* from I/JG 70. II *Gruppe* formed 6 April, 1940. All three *Gruppen* saw combat in Battle of Britain.

Zerstörergeschwader 76
I *Gruppe* with Bf110C saw combat in Poland and Norway, became II/JG 54, 6 April 1940. II *Gruppe* with Bf109 on North Sea coast until spring 1940, then equipped with Bf110C. III *Gruppe* formed from II/ZG 1. All three *Gruppen* saw combat in Battle of Britain. I *Gruppe* based at Stavanger. I *Gruppe* became II/NJG 1 September 1940. I/ZG 76 saw combat in the Balkans April/May 1941; 4 *Staffel* operating briefly in Iraqi colours, May 1941.

Jagdgeschwader 77
II *Gruppe* at Jever late 1939 with Bf109, and in Norway 10 April 1940. I *Gruppe* formed nucleus of IV/JG 51 from 15 August 1940 and based in France during Battle of Britain. II and III *Gruppen* saw combat in Balkans, April/May 1941.

Erprobungskommando 210
As *Erpr.Gr.* 210, activated July 1940, 1 and 2 *Staffel* with Bf110, 3 *Staffel* with Bf109. Saw combat in Battle of Britain and became *Schnellkampfgeschwader* 210 for the invasion of Russia.

Note: Honour titles were introduced at different periods; they are used here merely for identification.

THE AIRCRAFT

Messerschmitt Bf109D-1
Single-seat fighter in service at outbreak of war. Saw combat in Poland and North Sea coast 1939–early 1940. Served in second-line roles for some years.
Wingspan 32 ft 6 in *Length* 28 ft 7 in *Height* 8 ft 2½ in *Wing area* 176.5 sq ft *Weight loaded* 5,335 lb *Armament* 4 × 7.9 mm MG 17 machine guns, 2 in fuselage, 2 in wings *Powerplant* one Junkers Jumo 610D of 670 hp *Speed* 255 mph at 20,000 ft *Ceiling* 29,530 ft *Normal range* 385 miles.

Messerschmitt Bf109E-1 (Data in parentheses relates to E-3)
Single-seat day fighter and fighter-bomber. Mainstay of fighter arm 1939 to mid-1941; some 20 sub-variants saw service.
Wingspan 32 ft 5½ in *Length* 28 ft 10½ in *Height* 8 ft 5½ in *Wing area* 172.84 sq ft *Weight loaded* 5,667 lb (5,747 lb) *Armament* 4 × 7.9 mm MG 17 machine guns, 2 in wings, 2 in fuselage (2 × 20 mm MG FF cannon in wings, 2 × 7.9 mm MG 17 in fuselage) *Powerplant* one Daimler-Benz 601A of 1,100 hp *Speed* 310.7 mph at 19,865 ft *Ceiling* 33,790 ft *Range* 323 miles.

Messerschmitt Bf110C-1
Two/three seat day fighter and fighter bomber in service 1939–41.
Wingspan 53 ft 3¾ in *Length* 39 ft 7¼ in *Height* 13 ft 6½ in *Wing area* 413.334 sq ft *Weight loaded* 13,289 lb *Armament* 2 × 20 mm MG FF cannon and 4 × 7.9 mm machine guns in fuselage nose and 1 × 7.9 mm MG 15 machine gun on flexible mounting in rear cockpit section *Powerplant* two Daimler-Benz DB 601A-1s rated at 1,100 hp *Speed* 326 mph at 13,120 ft *Ceiling* 32,810 ft *Normal range* 565 miles.

LÉGENDES

1 Bf109E-1 apparemment du I/JG-1 juste avante le début de la guerre. Couleur vert foncé intégral et insignes nationaux typiques d'avant guerre. 2 Bf109E-1 avec des insignes d'arc et flèche du 7/JG 51, photographié quelque temps avant l'invasion de la Pologne, en train de faire le plein d'essence d'un camion-citerne. 3 Messerschmitts du 7/JG 51; l'avion au premier plan a des marques blanches et l'emblème de fuselage arrière du III Gruppe. 4 Un Bf109E-1 impeccable avec un emblème du II/JG 54 sur le nez; notez le poignet démarreur du moteur. 5 Des chasseurs bimoteurs Bf110C alignés devant l'usine avant livraison. 6 Une remise en état importante d'un Bf110C. 7 Les canons du nez d'un Bf110C—deux mitrailleuses 7.92 mm et deux canons 20 mm; bien que redoutables, cet armement pouvait rarement servir avantageusement à cause de la lenteur de l'appareil. 8 Bf109E avec un emblème du 'Richthofen Geschwader'—J2—sous la carlingue. 9 Le numéro élevé peint sur le fuselage arrière indique que ce Bf109E sert avec une unité d'instruction. 10 La carlingue serrée d'un Bf109E; notez que les instruments ont été modifiés légèrement pour les besoins de pilotes britanniques d'essai sur cet appareil capturé.

11 et 12 Le châssis étroit et peu solide du Bf109, et son habitude de dévier méchamment pendant le décollage et l'atterrissage occasionna beaucoup d'accidents pendant l'instruction. 13 Bf109E probablement du JG2, avec ce qui semble être un emblème personnel sous la forme de 'Popeye the Sailorman' peint sous la carlingue. 14 Quatre Bf109E-1s du Staffel, JG2 'Richthofen' en vol; le camouflage est maintenant limité à partie supérieure du fuselage seulement. Les chiffres sont en blanc, et l'emblème du Staffel, 'Bonzo the Dog' est à peine visible au-dessus des échappements. 15 Bf110Cs du Lehrgeschwader 1, avec des lettres de code L1 + CL + AL, + KL et + LL la troisième lettre est en jaun à chaque fois. Trois de ces avions ont un camouflage tacheté grossièrement pulvérisé sur les côtés et empennages en bleu ciel. 16 Messerschmitts du III/JG 51 sur un terrain d'aviation français, 1940. L'avion le plus éloigné a le symbole du chevron et circle d'un officier Technique d'escadron, et l'emblème du Gruppe sous la carlingue. Le plus près a l'emblème du chat noir du 8/JG 51 sur le capot. 17 et 18 Un camouflage tacheté intéressant sur le nez d'un Bf109E écrasé, côtes de la Manche, 1940; notez aussi les bouts des ailes blancs. 18 Bf109E tirant sur un ballon à air au-dessus de Douvres, août 1940. 19 Deux officiers Luftwaffe fument à côté d'un Bf109E endommagé, notez que l'avion est appuyé contre un tas de sacs de lest et il a un train d'atterrissage abimé. 20 Bf110Cs d'une unité de chasseurs bombardiers Erprobungsgruppe 210, qui spécialisa dans des raids osés très rapides pendant la Bataille d'Angleterre. Les lettres de codes du fuselage sont S9+.

21 Des pilotes du JG53 discutent d'une sortie au-dessus de la Manche. 22 Bf109E-3s au-dessus de la Côte anglaise; ceux-ci pourraient être des appareils du II/JG 3. 23 Un emblème du I/JG 52 sur le capot du Bf109E descendu en Angleterre août 1940. 24 et 25 Pilot Officier Wicks No 56 Sqn. RAF, inspecte le Bf109E-3 du 6/JG 51 qu'il descendit le 24 août 1940. L'emblème du II/JG 51 est peint sur le fuselage. 26 Bf109E-4 du Stab II/JG 3 'Udet' descendu à Kent le 5 septembre 1940; on croit généralement que c'était l'avion de Franz von Werra. 27 et 28 Bf110C-3, W. Nr. 1372, U8+HL du 3/ZG 26 'Horst Wessel' piloté par F.W.

Brinkmann et Uffz Krupshow, atterrissant brutalement à Lenham, Kent, le 11 septembre 1940. 29 Oberstleutnant Joachim-Friedrich Hüth le vétéran de la Première Guerre Mondiale, qui n'avait qu'une jambe, commanda ZG 26 à la Bataille d'Angleterre. 30 Une photo confuse mais intéressante d'un Bf109E avec des marques d'un officier Technique Gruppe, au-dessus de la Manche, 1940. Le fuselage et une partie de l'empennage sont presque complètement couverts d'un camouflage tacheté.

31 Une belle étude d'un Bf109E du JG53; notez le capot de couleur sans doute jaune, et l'emblème de l'unité—aussi la grande plaque d'acier amenagée dans le dessus de la carlingue sur des modèles subséquents du Bf109E. 32 Un Bf110C se prépare à décoller; après 1940 le Bf110 n'était plus considéré sérieusement comme chasseur de jour. 33 et 34 Des photos montrant un pilote, qu'on pense doit se nommer Nocker—du 1/JG 1 basé à De Kooy, Hollande au printemps de 1941. Notez les bouts blancs des ailes et du gouvernail; aussi le gilet de sauvetage en Kapok à l'ancienne mode. Dans la petite photo il montre du doigt un trou reprisé fait par une balle. 35 Bf109Es d'une unité non identifiée avec des marques II Gruppe. Notez les visées télescopiques débordant à travers les parebrises des deux machines les plus près; Adolf Galland utilisa un de ces artifices. 36 Bf110D-3 du 1/Zg 26 au-dessus de la Grèce, 1941. 37, 38 Un avion du 7 Staffel, JG 26 'Staffel Coeur Rouge' en Sicile 1941. 39 Bien que probablement photographié en Russie, fin 1941, ce Bf109E a ce type de lance-bombes ETC-50 et porte quarte bombes de 50 kilos—utilisé aussi par 'Jabos' sur les côtes de la Manche.

Notes sur les planches en couleurs

Page 25: Major d'une unité de chasseurs Luftwaffe, 1940, portant un uniforme facultatif en blanc d'été. Une bande bleue au bras avec le nom de son escadron 'Jagdgeschwader Richthofen' peut être, est portée au dessus du poignet droit. Des médailles comprennent la Croix de Fer 1ère et 2e classe, la Croix Espagnole et quelques médailles de service. Il porte un attribut de pilote et un attribut noir de blessé, 3e classe sur la poitrine gauche, et un attribut d'aigle en métal blanc accroché à droite. Des épaulettes et écussons du col sont renforcés de jaune de l'arme du service.

Page 26 en haut: Bf110C-1 du 2/ZG 76 Pologne, September 1939. Camouflage réglementaire en deux tons de vert 70 et 71 sur les surfaces supérieures 'M8' est le code Geschwader—'D' le code de l'avion individuel et 'K' le code 'Staffel' Le'D' est en rouge qui identifie le second Staffel de chaque Gruppe. Le détail indique l'emblème 'Locomotivstaffel' adopté par 1/ZG 76 comme résultat des succès des attaques de mitrailleuses sur des trains en Pologne; les codes du 1/ZG 76 se termineraient en 'H' au lieu de 'K'. **Page 26 en bas:** Bf109E-3 du 3/JG 51 hiver 1939–40. Camouflage dans des teints 70 et 71 sur toutes les surfaces en haut et sur les côtés; notez les grands insignes nationaux. Le numéro individuel de l'avion '3' est en jaune qui identifie le troisième Staffel de chaque Gruppe. L'emblème chamois est celui du Gruppe 1/JG 51, et la 'main jaune' est celui du Staffel.

Page 27: Bf109E-4 piloté par Lieutenant Waldemar ('Hein') Wübke du 9/JG 54; Guines, France, septembre 1940. Combinaison de couleurs typique dela fin de 1940; les surfaces bleues de côtés sont tachetées de gris ou vert. Le camouflage éclaté sur les surfaces en haut semble être en vert no. 70 et gris no.02 au lieu de la combinaison habituelle 70 et 71. Derrière la marque en croix sur le fuselage se trouve l'emblème qui identifie III Gruppe; le 'diable' sur le nez est l'emblème Staffel. L'attribut sous la carlingue est celui d'un chemin de fer allemand, et l'inscription indique 'Dans le service aérien des Chemins de Fer de l'Etat'. Ceci est une plaisanterie sarcastique se référant à la façon que les pilotes chasseurs fussent obligés de piloter tout près des bombardiers (c'est à dire, devenir des conducteurs de trains) plutôt que d'avoir la liberté de rechercher l'ennemi là où ils voulaient.

Page 28 et 29: Bf109E-1 piloté par Oberleutnant G. Framm, Staffelkapitän, 2/JG 27 début 1940, à la frontière franco-allemande. Le camouflage est apparemment dans des teints 70 et 02. Le numéro 1 individuel était souvent utilisé par le Staffelkapitän à cette date, mais l'habitude devenait rapidement impopulaire—cela le distingua trop pour l'ennemi. La couleur rouge des masques indique le deuxième Staffel de chaque Gruppe. Le drapeau de fer sur l'antenne de radio et la rayure autour du fuselage sont tous deux des signaux de commandes typiques de cette période mais bientôt abandonnés. Le nom SAMOA sur le nez rappelle une coutume commencée par le premier Kommander du 1/JG 2 Hauptmann Riegel—chaque avion dans le Staffel portait le nom d'une ancienne colonie allemande.

Page 30: Bf110C-3 du 3/ZG 2; Amiens, septembre 1940—Le camouflage et les marques sont normaux mais notez les parties couvertes de peinture où des marques précédentes ont été recouvertes. A l'origine cet avion vola avec 1/ZG 52, dont le code était 'A2' et l'emblème du dragon est illustré ici. Après les machines du 1/ZG 52 ont été repris par ZG2 mais beaucoup retenaient toujours leurs anciennes marques.

Page 31 en haut: Des emblèmes des unités chasseurs: (1) 9/JG 2 (2) Stab/JG 1 (3) Stab, III/JG 26 (4) ZG (5) JG 26 (6) 1/JG 54. **Page 31 en bas:** Kfz 12 (Mercedes Benz 230) 4 × 2 voiture de campagne, utilisée par du personnel du 9/JG 26 comme voiture tous usages dans le Pas de Calais, été 1940. L'emblème de l'unité est en blanc; le détail montre que le style dans lequel il apparaîssait sur l'avion dans cet escadron.

Page 32 à gauche: Pilote chasseur été 1940. Il porte une casque légère en tulle et un gilet de sauvetage et ces bottes de pilotes par-dessus ses pantalons et sa chemise de tenue journalière. Des cartouches à fusée éclairante sont portées en bandolières autour des bottes. **Page 32 à droite:** Unteroffizier mécanique, 1940 portant des bleus de travail réglementaires en noire en un calot de tenue journalière. Le seul insigne est le Tresse argent de rang de sous-officier autour du col.

ÜBERSCHRIFT

1 Bf109E-1 vermutlich vom I/JG 1, kurz vor Kriegsausbruch Dunkelgrüne Anstrich, typische vorkriegs-Nationalkrokarden. **2** Ein Bf109E-1, mit dem Pfeil und Bogen Abzeichen vom 7/JG 51, beim Tanken. Das Bild wurde kurz vor dem Angriff auf Polen gemacht. **3** Messerschmitts vom 7/JG 51. Das Flugzeug im Vordergrund hat weisse Abzeichen und das Rumpfhinterteil-emblem der III Gruppe. **4** Nagelneue Bf109E-1 mit dem Emblem des II/JG 54 an der Rumpfspitze Der Anlasshebel beinerken! **5** Eine Bf110C zweimotorige Jagdmaschinen vor der Fabrik. **6** Eine Bf110C wird eine Überholung unterzogen. **7** Rumpfspitzen. Bewaffnung einer Bf110C—zwei 7.92 mm M-Gs und zwei 20 mm Kanonen. Obwohl sehr stark, kam diese Bewaffnung wegen der Trägheit des Flugzeugs, nur Selten zum Tragen. **8** Bf109E mit Waffen des 'Richthofen Geschwaders'—JG2—interm Kanzel. **9** Die Nummer, hoch an den Rumpfhinterteil dieser Bf109E angebracht, bedeutet 'Ausbildungseinheit'. **10** Der enge Kanzel einer Bf109E. Sie ist eine Beute-Maschine deshalb die Umgestaltung der Instrumente für britische Test-Piloten.

11 et 12 Die Bf109 hatte schwache, schmale Fahrgestell und eine starke Ausschweiftendenz beim Starten und handen. Sie verursachte viele Unfälle beim Pilotenausbildung. **13** Eine Bf109E, vermutlich vom JG.2. Uterm Kanzel erscheint 'Popeye the Sailorman'—wahrscheinlich das persönliche Emblem des Piloten. **14** Vier Bf109E-1's vom 1. Staffel, JG2 'Richthofen'. Tarnfarben werden jetzt nur auf den Oberflächen getragen. Die Zifferrnn sind weiss und das Staffelemblem 'Bonzo the Dog' ist gerade über die Auspuffrohre sichtbar. **15** Bf110Cs vom Lehrgeschwader 1 mit Erkennungsbuchstaben L1+CL, +AL, +KL und +LL in jedem Falle ist die dritte Buchstabe gelb. Drei dieser Maschinen haben grobe gefleckte Tarnanstriche über die hellblaue Rumpfseiten und Schwanzteile. **16** Messerschmitts vom III/JG 51 auf einem französischen Flugplatz, 1940. Das Flugzeug im Hintergrund tragt das Winkel und Kreisemblem eines Staffel-Ingenieurs dazn das Gruppenemblem unterm Kanzel. Die vorderste Maschine trägt auf der Motorhaube die schwarze Katze—Emblem vom 8/JG 51. **17** Diese abgeschossene Bf109E auf der Kanalkuste, 1940 hat ein interessante gefleckte Rumpfspitzentarnfarbenschema. Die weisse Flügelspitzen sind auch zu beachten. **18** Eine Bf109E greift eine Luftballon über Dover, August 1940 an. **19** Zwei Luftwaffe Offiziere nehmen eine Zigarettenpause bei einer beschädigten Bf109E. Die Sandsack-Unterstützing and das gebogene Fahrgestell beachten! **20** Bf110Cs einer JaBo Einheit, Erprobungs gruppe 210, die sich als tollkühne Stippangriff-spezialisten während der Luftschlacht über England bewährten. Rumpferkennungsbuchstaben: 'S9+'.

21 Piloten vom JG53 'PikAs' Unterhalten sich über einem einsatz über dem Kanal. **22** Bf109E-3s über die Englische Kuste Diese Maschinen sind Wahrscheinlich vom II/JG 3. **23** Motorhaubenemblem des I/JG 52 auf einer Bf109E, die über England, August 1940 abgeschossen wurde. **24 & 25** Pilot Officer Wicks, No56 Sqn RAF nimmt eine Bf109-E vom 6/JG 51, die er am 24.August 1940 abgeschossen hat in augenschein. Das

Rumpfemblem ist vom II/ JG 51. **26** Diese Bf109E-4 vom Stab, II/JG 3 'Vdet', über Kent am 5.September 1940 ist dem Pilot Franz von Werra zugeschrieben. **27 & 28** Diese Bf110C-3, W. Nr. 1372, U8 + HL vom 3/ZG 26 'Horst Wessel', Besatzung Fw. Brinkmann und Uffz. Krupshow machte bei Lenham, Kent, am 11. September 1940 eine Bauchlandung. **29** Oberstleutnant Joachim-Friedrich Hüth, einbeiniger Flieger-As vom 1. Weltdrieg, der Kommandeur der ZG26 während der Luftschlacht über England war. **30** Ein etwas unklares aber interessantes Bild einer Bf109E mit den Markierungen eines Gruppen-Ingenieurs über den Aermel-Kanal, 1940. Der Rumpf und Teile des Schwanzstückes sind fast überall mit gefleckten Tarnfarben überstrichen worden.

31 Hervorragendes Bild einer Bf109E vom JG53. Die Motorenhaube (vermutlich gelb) und das Staffelemblem sowie die Kanzelhaubepanzerung, die auf den späteren Bf109Es eingeführt worden war, breachten! **32** Eine Bf110C bei der Start-Vorbereitung. Nach 1940 wurde die Bf110 nicht mehr als Tageseinsatzfähig in der Jagdrolle berechnet. **33 & 34** Aufnahmen eines Piloten (Namens Nocker?) vom I/JG 1; Heimatflugplatz De Kooy, Holland, Frühling 1941. Die weissen Flügelspitzen. Schwanzfloss und die altmodische Kapok-Rettungs-weste beachten. Im kleineren Bild dentet er an einem ausgebesserten Kugelloch hin. **35** Bf109Es in der Tracht der II Gruppe (Einheit unbekannt). Die Fernzelröhre, die durch die Windschutzscheiben der zwei Maschinen im Vordergrund durchzustossen scheinen, beachten! Adolf Galland hat einer diesen Vorrichtungen benutzt. **36** Bf110D-3 vom I/ZG 26 über Griechenland, 1941. **37 & 38** Maschinen vom 7. Staffel, JG26— 'Rotherz-Staffel'-Sizilien, 1941. **39** Dieses Bild stammt vermutlich aus Russland, Herbst 1941 Die Maschine, eine Bf109E hat aber die Bombenbehälter—Type ETC-50, mit einer Tragfähigkeit von vier Bomben X50kg-wie von den Jabos über die Aermel-Kanal Kuste benutzt wurden.

Farbafeln

Seite 25: Ein Major einer Luftwaffe Kampfeinheit, 1940. Er trägt die weisse Sommeruniform die jenach belieben getragen werden Konnte. Der blaue Aermelband mit Ehrentitel 'Jagdgeschwader Richthofen' wurde rechts getragen. Unter den Oden erkennt man das Eiserne Kreuz 1. und 2. Klasse, das Spanien-Kreuz und einige Feldzugsorden. Er trägt das Pilotenabzeichen und, links an der Brust das Verwundertenabzeichen 3. Klasse in schwarz. Rechts trägt er ein Adlerabzeichen in silber. Die Kragenspiegel und Schulterstücke haben gelben Futter = Fliegerbranche.

Seite 26 (Oben): Ein Bf110C-1 vom 2/ZG 76, Polen, September 1939. Vorschrifts-mässige Splitter Tarnfarbenschema in hell- und dunkelgrün—70 und 71—zu den Oberflächen. Geschwaderkennzeichen—'M8'; Flugzeugbuchstabe—'D'; Staffelbuchstabe—'K' Die 'D' ist rot (d.h. 2. Staffel jeder Gruppe). Das kleine Bild zeigt das 'Locomotiv-staffel' Emblem, dass vom I/ZG 76 nach erfolgreiche Eisenbahnvernichtungseinsätze in Polen adoptiert worden ist. Die Erkennungschiffre vom I/ZG 76 wurde 'H' statt 'K' als Endbuchstabee haben. **Seite 26 (Unten):** Eine Bf109E-3 vom 3/JG 51, Winter 1939–40

Tarnfarben (Schatten 70 und 71) über sämtlich[…] Seitenflächen. Die grosse Hoheitsabzeichen b[…] Flugzeugnummer, 'Z' ist gelb d.h. die dritte Staffe[…] Das Chamois-Emblem ist das Gruppenemblem[…] gelbe Hand' ist vom Staffel.

Seite 27: Bf109E-4, vom Leutnant Waldemar ('[…] 9/JH 54 geflogen; Guines, Frankreich, Sep[…] Typische Farbenschema vom Herbst 1940: die[…] und Schwanzseiten sind mit grau oder grün über[…] Die Splitter Tarnung auf den Oberflächen schein[…] und grau Nr20 statt den herkömmlichen 70-un[…] nation zu sein. Hinter dem Rumpf Balkend[…] Emblem der III Gruppe. Der 'Teufel' an der Rum[…] Staffelemblem. Das Wappen unterm Kanze[…] Deutschen Reichsbahn; der Wahlspruch ist e[…] Wilz über die Einsatzmethode, wonach die Jagd[…] Begleitung zu den Bomber (d.h. praktisch 'Zugf[…] fliegen mussten, trotz der Freiheit, um den Fein[…] und zu bekämpfen zu haben.

Seite 28–29: Bf109E-1, von Oberleutant G. [...] kapitän 2/JG 27 Frühfahr 1940, an der deutsch[…] Grenze. Die Tarnfarben scheinen Nr70 und Nr[…] Flugzeugnummer '1' wurde oft von dem Sta[…] dieser Zeit benutzt; die Sitte wurde bald aufgege[…] Feinde sehr schnell ausgesucht wurde! Die[…] ungsfarbe bedeutet den zweiten Staffel jeder[…] metalle Wimpel an der Antenne und die S[…] Rumpfherum sind beide typische 'Befehlsha[…] dieser Zeit, die bald im Wegfall kamen. Die Na[…] der Rumpfspitze führt und an einer Sitte zurück,[…] Kommandeur des I/JG 27, Hauptmann Rieg[…] wurde, indem jedes Flugzeug des Staffels d[…] ehemaligen deutsche Kolonie trug.

Seite 30: Bf110C-3 vom 3/ZG 2; Amiens, Septem[…] Tarnfarben und Markierungen sind herkömmlic[…] überstrichenen ehemalige Markierungen sind zu[…] Flugzeug diente vorher beim I/ZG 52 dessen Chy[…] dessen Drachenemblem hier abgebildet ist. Nach der Einverleibung der Maschinen vom I/ZC[…] trugen viele ihre alte Markierungen weiter.

Seite 31 (Oben): Emblemen Verschiedenen Jag[…] 9/JG (2) Stab/JG 1 (3) Stab III/JG 26 (4) ZG2[…] I/JG 54. **Seite 31 (Unten):** Kfz 12 (Mercedes B[…] Feldwagen, vom Personal des 9/JG 26, als 'Mäd[…] im Pas-de-Calais, Sommer, 1940 benutzt. Das Ein[…] weiss. Das kleine Bild zeigt die Art der Anbring[…] Staffel.

Seite 32 (Links): Jagdflieger, Sommer 1940. […] Fliegerhelm aus leichtem Netztoff, vorschrifts[…] tungsweste und Fliegerstiefel über seinem no[…] themd und Hosen. Um seinem Stiefel sind Leucht[…] in Bandoliere um gebundem. **Seite 32 (Rechts):** […] Mechaniker, 1940. Er trägt vorschriftsmassige[…] leidung und Schiffschen. Das einzige Abzeichen i[…] Uteroffiziers Dienstgradtressen um den Kragen.